FORGIVENESS
THE PATH TO HAPPINESS

FORGIVENESS
THE PATH TO HAPPINESS

SANDRA SUMMERFIELD KOZAK, M.S.

HIMALAYAN INSTITUTE®
PRESS
HONESDALE, PENNSYLVANIA, USA

Himalayan Institute Press
952 Bethany Turnpike
Honesdale, PA 18431

www.HimalayanInstitute.org
© 2005 The Himalayan International Institute of Yoga
Science and Philosophy of the U.S.A.®
09 08 07 06 05
6 5 4 3 2 1

Printed in China

The paper used in this publication meets the minimum
requirements of American National Standard for
Information Sciences—Permanence of Paper for Printed
Library Materials, ANSI Z39.48-1984.

Library of Congress Cataloging-in-Publication Data

Kozak, Sandra Summerfield.
  Forgiveness : the path to happiness / Sandra
Summerfield Kozak.
    p. cm.
  Includes bibliographical references.
  ISBN-13: 978-0-89389-252-4 (trade pbk. : alk. paper)
  ISBN-10: 0-89389-252-1 (trade pbk. : alk. paper)
  1. Forgiveness. 2. Happiness. I. Title.

BF637.F67K69 2005
158.2—dc22   2005012490

for my parents
Opal and Charles Cook

CONTENTS

FOREWORD

Everyone wants to be happy. But what, exactly, are they looking for? Wise men have debated the nature of happiness for centuries. The concept has been incorporated into the American Dream, into the concept of heaven, and into the marketplace as the reward for almost every product. In fact, the quest for happiness motivates almost all our actions. But few can say that they are really happy.

Why is this so hard? When we think we have found happiness, why does it fade so quickly? We look everywhere for The Answer, but it always eludes us. In this small book Sandra Summerfield Kozak answers these questions in the light of ancient wisdom proven over time. And like any great truth, once you hear it, you realize that, deep down, you have always known it.

The author writes from both knowledge and experience. A scholar of the ancient texts and a student of Western psychology for over 20 years, she reminds us that lasting happiness lies in learning to forgive those who have hurt us, that wisdom is already ours. It's inside us always, but it has been pushed to the background while we deal with the cacophony of daily life. "Bitterness, anger, resentment, and blame" she writes, "are like the four walls of a prison cell. Its door can be opened only by forgiving. As long as we are tied to a situation that keeps us locked in negative emotions, we are stuck in the role of helpless victim, at the mercy of other people's misdeeds." If we can just let go of the past, she continues, we will be happy in the present.

Forgiveness is written for all of us—teachers, students, and especially those who are suffering and willing to look at the world in a new way. The opening chapters tell us what forgiveness is and what happens to us if we don't forgive. Subsequent chapters tell us how we can eliminate negative thoughts and feelings and let go of expectations and attachments. The chapter on relationships centers on understanding. Clear, practical instructions for creating change accompany every section.

In short, this book is a gift. Everyone who wants to be happy can benefit from its wisdom. By acting on its simple, practical advice, we can be certain that we are on the path to happiness.

Lillian Dangott, Ph.D.
Psychologist
Professor Emeritus
University of Nevada, Reno

ACKNOWLEDGEMENTS

Many people have helped this book along in its journey to completion, including the psychologists and physicians who read the manuscript and generously gave their support and suggestions—Jerry Harrison, Seanna Adamson, Sharon Cottor, Elgin Heinz, and especially Lillian Dangott.

The book is here because of the insight, enthusiasm, and extraordinary expertise of Anne Craig, Anna Ketterhagen, and the whole staff at the Himalayan Institute Press who made the process go so smoothly. It could not have come into existence without the unfaltering support of Pandit Rajmani Tigunait and Deborah Willoughby.

My appreciation also goes to Jill McQuillin, Sheila Bishop, and Suzanne Al Nour for their unfaltering encouragement and love when it was most needed.

My heartfelt thanks to all of you—and especially to my husband and best friend, Peter Ciriscioli.

THE JOURNEY

Since the beginning of recorded time, human beings have searched for happiness—not just fleeting moments of pleasure, but an abiding, unshakeable happiness that lasts a lifetime and transcends the suffering intrinsic to living life. To this end, philosophers and holy men sat by the river in the Indus Valley thousands of years ago and meditated on the age-old question of how to sail through the hardships of life and end suffering. In the process, they discovered a state of calm repose that could be created at will, one that would carry people through all of life's experiences.

As the ancient yoga masters pursued this issue of happiness, they found that past discord continues to affect us long after an event has taken place. They discovered that thoughts and emotions that were not fully resolved at the time of discord are stored in the body's chemistry and buried in the deeper levels of the mind. And they saw that we unconsciously spend energy holding down emotional memories when we try not to see or feel the unresolved past.

The yoga masters also saw that these hidden forces keep us from being objective and cause unconscious, automatic reactions in our psyches. So they developed practices to remove veiled past experiences from the invisible recesses of the mind and bring them to a visible conscious level where they can be released forever. By removing them, they discovered, we gain new energy as well as the freedom to respond to current situations openly instead of remaining victim to our invisible past.

The ancient yoga masters passed down techniques for seeing ourselves as we really are, releasing mental blocks to happiness, letting go of negative feelings, and forgiving the past. And today, through the practices contained in the vast system of yoga, we can move ourselves from a negative to a positive position physically, mentally, emotionally, and spiritually—and achieve abiding happiness. This makes yoga a highly effective system of psychology that is straightforward and user friendly. And within its practical system for handling life, yoga is a step-by-step method for freeing people from suffering, anger, resentment, and pain.

Yoga has been passed down for thousands of years— at first orally from teacher to student and then through terse aphorisms known as Patanjali's *Yoga Sutra*. To the surprise of modern psychologists, this ancient text describes the functions of the mind and the interplay between them. It is uncannily accurate. In fact, the basis for many modern psychological techniques can be found here—grounding, reframing, refocusing, meaning held in context, empowerment through dignity, experience-generated meaning, strengthening through ethical behavior, reality as a choice, and the impossibility of finding objective reality—to name just a few.

Yoga psychology removes the veil that stops us from

feeling compassion, love, and the connection we have with our whole being. Does it work? Yoga has weathered thousands of years and is still here because it is so effective. It has stood the test of time. It does work—not only as a way of thinking, but also as a technique for dealing with life's problems.

forgiveness—IT'S NECESSARY

- Forgiveness is necessary because we can't have abiding happiness without it.

- Forgiveness is necessary because we can't have abiding good health without it.

- Forgiveness is necessary because it improves our relationships and interactions.

- Forgiveness is necessary because it quiets anger and resentment.

- Forgiveness is necessary because it clears the mind/body of thoughts and feelings from past events.

- Forgiveness is necessary because life is not fair and unwanted things will happen.

- Forgiveness is necessary because we can't enjoy the present moment without it.

- Forgiveness is necessary for getting what we want.

chapter one

*A*BOUT FORGIVENESS

HOW DOES YOGA PSYCHOLOGY apply to forgiveness? Perfectly. The ancient yogis knew that when we cannot forgive others or ourselves, or when we cannot detach from anger and pain, we are stuck. And they found that being stuck in emotions and thoughts associated with past events does not allow us to fully experience the present moment or the joy that living with an open heart has to offer. Yoga's ancient wisdom frees people's minds and hearts by helping them to understand themselves, develop a whole new perspective on life, strengthen their self-esteem, detach from fear, and create a fine focus on what is really important to their lives. These are the same skills that are required for forgiveness.

Forgiveness is the process of letting go, and it is necessary for us to learn to do this if we want to manage our response to conflict and live happy lives. Unfortunately, however, few of us have been taught anything about the process, and most of us haven't yet learned what forgiveness is.

Forgiveness is the feeling of peace we experience when we are able to release our attachment to past offenses and rest in full acceptance of the present moment. We can do this easily when life is flowing smoothly, but in times of strain and conflict we lose control of our peaceful, pleasurable state.

But conflict is an inevitable part of life, and when discord or conflict arises, so do emotions like anger, depression, fear, anxiety, guilt, and insecurity. Besides making us vulnerable to negative emotions, conflict also exposes us to rejection, blame, manipulation, and the pain we feel from damaged or broken relationships. We may not be able to avoid discord, but we can avoid reacting negatively to it. And we can shorten the length of time we think about it.

We can gain control over how we feel and the choices we make by repeatedly going through the process of letting go and forgiving, and we can learn to do this through understanding and experience. It is not easy, but the more we go through the process, the easier it gets. It is like having a forgiveness muscle. Without use, the muscle is small and weak, but as we exercise it the muscle becomes stronger, larger, and easier to identify. Likewise, every repetition of the forgiveness process strengthens our ability to forgive and makes it faster and easier for us to let go of pain and negativity.

Bitterness, anger, resentment, and blame are like the four walls of a prison cell. Its door can be opened only by forgiving. As long as we are tied to a situation that keeps us locked in negative emotions, we are stuck in the role of helpless victim, at the mercy of other people's misdeeds.

Forgiveness allows us to let go of our negative emotions and release ourselves from their prison. When we withhold forgiveness and nurse resentment, we give away control of our health and well-being. Through forgiveness we can elect to have happy lives.

Anger—the Biggest Obstacle

Anger is normal and natural. What we do with anger is what is important. There are four ways to deal with it: denial, expression, exploration, and forgiveness.

- Denial keeps us locked in silent resentment and bitterness, and carrying unexpressed anger around with us closes our hearts and deadens our experience of life.

- Expressing our feelings can be problematic. It is healthy to be aware of angry feelings, and anger can help us protect and assert ourselves as well as establish boundaries, but expressing anger is usually damaging to us. It may be appropriate for a short period of time, but it will create problems with our health, our work, and our relationships with others if it continues.

- Exploring the feelings that lie beneath anger can be productive. Anger is often only a "surface" emotion, and we feel better when we learn what our feelings really are and how they are triggered. In yoga, the study of ourselves (svadhyaya) is fundamental for walking the path of personal freedom.

- Forgiveness is the most benign and effective way to deal with anger (and the associated desire for revenge) directly. When we can relieve ourselves of harmful thoughts and feelings, we are able to direct our choices—and, consequently, our lives.

According to Webster's *New World Dictionary,* forgive means "to give up resentment against or the desire to punish; stop being angry with; pardon; to give up all claim to punish or exact penalty for an offense; to overlook."

Booker T. Washington is an extraordinary example of one who maintained control of his daily life through forgiveness. His motto was, "I shall not allow any man to belittle my soul by making me hate him." A slave who began working as a small child, he directed his energy toward improving his life instead of becoming a victim to poverty, slavery, or child labor. He did not allow injustice, complacency, hostility, or condescension to soil his experience. In his remarkable life,

Booker T. Washington was a great success, not just because he founded the Tuskegee Institute, was an advisor to three presidents, and became a teacher at the first African-American college in America, but also because he was able to continually choose happiness and freedom in his own mind, heart, and life.

Forgiveness is a choice that flows from a decision. It doesn't happen on its own. First, we must decide we will choose happiness and freedom over pain and anger. We must decide that we will choose to live in the present moment. And then, in every situation that confronts us, we must enforce our decision by repeatedly making the choice to let go of our anger and forgive. Like Booker T. Washington, we need to always remember that forgiving keeps us in control of our lives.

Eliminating Negativity

Forgiveness begins when we make the choice to reduce or eliminate negative feelings, thoughts, and behavior toward the offender or ourselves. This may not immediately remove all of the hurting and sorrow we experience, but as we practice forgiveness the pain becomes more bearable and our minds less obsessed with the past.

Further along in the forgiving process, we begin to let go of painful experiences and gain the ability to choose our life's direction rather than let the past direct us. To do this, we must forgive small and large transgressions alike. Then, through the process of forgiving, we begin to learn about ourselves. We learn to take responsibility for our feelings, to understand that our expectations and attachments may lead us to take things too personally, to reduce the need for other people to behave in particular ways. We learn to rewrite our grievance story so that it becomes one of good intentions—and thus change our expectations into hopes or wishes.

We may not be aware that we have any problems right this minute, but that doesn't mean we don't need to learn to forgive. Over the course of our lives, discord sometimes arises that has not been fully resolved. We may only think about the problem occasionally, but it continues to exist somewhere in the deeper levels of our minds. And years later, this unresolved, repressed negativity can still close our hearts and alter our thinking. We may not be aware that pain and resentment color our lives, and we not may be aware that some of our decisions and actions are centered on evading the possibility of duplicating past painful experiences. But this is how dormant emotional past events can redirect the choices we make every day of our lives. Ellen is a good example of the way an unconscious decision to avoid a second experience of loss determined her actions.

Ellen's father died when she was ten years old. In her adult years, her relationships with men were permeated by the unconscious fear that she would be left again. The more fully she connected to the man she was dating, the greater her fear became. And when her unconscious fear became too great, she would find something wrong with the man's behavior, create fights, blame him for the mess he had made of the relationship, and then leave in a cloud of justified indignation. She was completely unaware of the part she played in the event.

After years of repeating this pattern of behavior, Ellen fell in love with a man who disrupted her usual pattern, and she remained in this relationship long past her typical leaving time. Through it she gained awareness of her fearful feelings and saw her own behavior clearly for the first time. With subsequent therapy, Ellen learned that her unconscious fear that another man she loved would leave her, as her father had done, had repeatedly sabotaged her ideas, decisions, and relationships. She could see that her choices had been directed by past pain and an old unconscious decision never to be hurt like that

again. She forgave her father and let go of her
crippling fear of loss. Ellen soon met and married her husband of fifteen years.

Ellen's past experiences had been directing the
choices she thought she made freely. Stored emotional memories, however, like regret, hurt feelings, resentment, and anger, determine our perception and our
experience reactively. Past traumas continue to interfere with our ability to see a situation clearly or objectively, with our ability to trust others, and with our feelings of self-worth. They also greatly limit our
experience in the present moment.

When we can employ yoga practices for clearing the
past from the mind and body, our decisions about how
to handle today's experiences are less directed by unresolved traumas or offenses, and our ability to live in the
present moment as it is increases. Through the quieting
practice of meditation *(dhyana)*, the healthful balancing
of the yoga postures *(asanas)*, and the deep renewal that
comes from the practice of breath control *(pranayama)*,
the past is cleared from our minds and bodies and we
can enjoy better health, increased energy, and a renewed
sense of our connectedness to the totality of existence.

As our sense of "presence" grows, the quality of our
experience intensifies in a positive way; for each time
we are able to let go of some of our past traumas,
the energy that had been used to hold down those

experiences is freed and available to us. We begin to feel more energized and complete. We experience more self-confidence, more self-awareness, more ability to trust, and a stronger sense of well-being simply because we have released that part of the past that keeps us unconsciously reacting instead of consciously responding to people and situations.

The Gift of Forgiveness

Forgiving doesn't necessarily mean that we excuse or condone behavior that offends us. It simply means that we come to terms with what is happening—with the reality of the situation. It means letting go of how it "should have been." To accept reality as it is, we have to give up expecting or wanting things that other people are either incapable or unwilling to give us. Accepting what is true right now frees us from attachment to how things "should be," and our attachment is the primary source of our pain.

Forgiveness is about taking responsibility for our own happiness and making a better life for ourselves. It is solely for our own benefit. It is not about giving anything to the people who hurt us. It is not about giving up anything at all. If our relationship with the "offender" continues, it is because we think it is best for us. We need to make our decisions about forgiving based on the best way to take care of ourselves.

Because deciding to forgive releases us from pain

and anger, it is a gift we give to ourselves. When we choose to forgive, we are choosing to live in the present moment and leave the past behind us.

Forgiveness is for our own benefit. When we are hurt and upset, forgiveness makes us feel better. It increases our self-esteem, self-control, and emotional stability. It protects and strengthens our relationships with others. If we choose to hang on to resentment, we inadvertently hurt ourselves.

So we must recognize who is being hurt by non-forgiveness. The offenders are not staying awake at night, suffering upset stomachs and replaying the "wrongness" of the situation over and over again in their heads. We are. We are the hurt ones who need to be emancipated, especially if we are waiting for apologies or plotting revenge. We may want the offenders to lament their wrongdoing, but often they can't or they just won't. Either way, there is nothing we can do about their actions. Our wanting revenge only hurts us. And as long as we continue to insist that an external event (like their apology or some form of revenge) is what it takes to make us feel better, our bodies will continue to feel the hurt and anger. We are keeping it alive even though it makes us ill.

We begin to feel better when we start to let go and forgive. We are the ones most affected by the pain, and we are the ones who have the responsibility for changing our condition. Coming to terms with this responsibility is strengthening—and we are strong enough to make these changes. To guide our choices, all we need to do is investigate the offending situation and our reactions to it, widen our perspective, eliminate some of our expectations and outdated decisions, and commit to our own happiness.

When to Forgive

How do we know we need to practice forgiveness? When we replay the same scene over and over again in our minds, we know we are stuck and need to let go and forgive. If what we want to say to someone (or what we would say if we had the opportunity) is playing like a broken record in our minds, we know that we need to let go and forgive. If we retell our story over and over to everyone who will listen, or if we have imaginary conversations that justify our behavior or feelings, it is time to begin the letting go/forgiveness process. And if we begin to relish the idea of revenge (whether we plan on it or not), it is definitely time to begin.

Here are a few questions that will help you recognize and determine whether or not you need to practice forgiveness.

- Do you want to get even and make "them" pay for what they did (or didn't do)?

- Do you get angry every time you think about them and what they did (or didn't do)?
- Do you replay the offensive and painful behavior over and over again in your mind?
- Do you avoid seeing or talking with them?
- Do you think about the things you should have said or what they need to hear?
- Do you tell your story of what happened over and over again?
- Do you dwell in the past, adding up all the things that you don't like about them?

If the answer is "yes" to three or more questions, it's time to clean up some past issues and work on forgiving. If the answer is "yes" to five or more questions, it's definitely time to take care of your mental, physical, and emotional health and well-being and learn to forgive—NOW!

> Forgiving those who have caused us pain or sorrow is one of life's most difficult tasks, but we must forgive to keep our bodies healthy and our minds and spirits free.

We Don't Have to Lose

Forgiveness is not about giving up anything—except bad feelings. We can forgive and not even tell anyone that we are doing it. There are many things we don't have to do when we forgive. Here is a list of most of them. You can probably add more.

- We don't have to forget what happened or pretend it didn't happen.
- We don't have to give up our grieving or diminish our feelings of loss or pain.
- We don't have to excuse or condone selfish, rude, or abusive behavior.
- We don't have to become a doormat. Forgiveness is not weakness; it takes strength and courage to let go and forgive.
- We don't have to justify other people's behavior.
- We don't have to reconcile with anyone or renew our trust in them.
- We don't have to remain trapped in negative thoughts and feelings like anger, guilt, resentment, blame, shame, or pain.

It's not necessary to understand why someone acted as they did in order to forgive them. They may not even know why they said or did something hurtful. Understanding their motives, opinions, and concerns may help us widen our own perspective, but "why" information about them is not a prerequisite for forgiving.

To forgive, we need only to understand the situation that created the pain we are experiencing, know exactly how we feel about what happened, see our role in the interaction objectively, let go of all "shoulds" and "if onlys," and repeatedly focus on our commitment to happiness.

Three Levels of Forgiveness

If we don't feel like forgiving, we may have forgotten that we are responsible for our reactions in every situation. Remember: forgiveness is a learned process. Our ability to remember our responsibility and make the decision to forgive sharpens with time. There are' three levels of expertise in the art of knowing how to forgive.

Forgiveness begins when we realize that we feel awful when we are struggling with negative emotions and thoughts, that we want to choose how we respond to the behavior that is directed toward us, and that we want to put our own health and well-being first. At this level we begin to look at the offender's point of view and see the other side of the story. In time our justified anger is lessened and we can release the need to blame (ourselves, others, or the situation). In some instances we may decide we can let it go and just walk away from the problem. Practicing first on small grievances makes walking away easier. With larger conflicts, we may only be able to inch away slowly.

At the second level of forgiveness, we have begun to see the beneficial results of forgiving, and with practice we are now able to choose to forgive more easily and quickly. At this level we may feel hurt for a short time, but we can also see the bigger picture, quickly work though our grievance, or decide to just let it go. We know the value of forgiving and are more interested in practicing it. We know that the amount of time we spend in anger, hurt, or emotional pain is up to us. We know we are the decision makers.

At the third level, we have become even more proficient practitioners of forgiveness. Having gained some experience in accepting responsibility for our actions and working through our reactive choices, we can now begin to choose to forgive at the time the offense takes place. When conflict arises, we are able to look first to our reactions, knowing that we can choose happiness as our life experience.

Commitment to Happiness

Yoga is much more than the exercise, breathing, and relaxation practices found in many of today's classes. By studying and employing yoga psychology, we can understand the workings of our minds, further our self-exploration, and form a focused commitment that will free us to be the people we choose to be.

The practice of yoga psychology releases us from being victimized by our past and helps us recognize how to choose happiness by:

- widening our perspectives and releasing us from the effects of past painful feelings and thoughts;
- quieting our expectations and judgments;
- reducing or eliminating our attachment to other people's behavior; and
- creating a fine focus and commitment to what makes us feel good about our lives and ourselves.

chapter two

*I*F WE DON'T FORGIVE

THE ANCIENT YOGA MASTERS DISCOVERED that we can choose to be happy. When we follow the yogic path, they found, we learn to become one with the best part of ourselves—and this is the true definition of happiness. Yoga is an extraordinary guide for knowing ourselves, releasing restrictions, and living a happy life. The path of forgiveness, too, is a path of self-awareness and self-discovery. It intensifies the quality of our life experience and strengthens our sense of personal security and self-esteem. The path of forgiveness is the practice of yoga.

Conflict, however, is inherent in living. When it enters our lives, we can either let it go and forgive the offense or dig in and hold on to our position. When we are wrapped in emotional pain, however, we may become so caught up in our "justified" anger and resentment that we can't walk away from it.

But our health and happiness are affected by negative

thoughts and emotions. When we don't forgive, we become trapped in our feelings. We relive our past anger and hurt and become victim to a now-dead experience. And besides hurting ourselves, we are putting a strain on our relationships. So before we make the choice to live in this negative mire, let's look at just how much a self-righteous position will cost us. When we understand the price we pay for holding onto harmful thoughts and emotions, it can spur us on to begin the liberating process of forgiveness.

Adapt to Live

The work of Hans Selye, M.D., the father of the entire stress concept, shows that there is only so much adaptability available to the body/mind in one human life, and that the body, mind, and emotions must "adapt" to the stress of life every minute of every day. Each adaptation throws the body's chemistry into action (the fight-or-flight response) to prepare for the situation and to handle immediate change. The body can adapt many times in a lifetime—but it cannot adapt forever.

According to Dr. Selye, our health can be measured by how much reaction we have to any stressor, and when the body/mind can no longer make the next adaptation, there is death. The more reaction to stress, the more adaptation is required and the more energy is expended. Longevity can be measured by how often and how intense the demand for energy.

When we say to ourselves, "I can't accept this. I hate this. This will be the death of me," our resistant words place additional demands on our bodies and increase the need for adaptation. When we insist that life or behavior be the way we want it and dictate those ideas to ourselves and others, we are interfering with our own health and longevity. And the more demands we place on behavior (ours or other people's), the more our minds and bodies will have to adapt. Without knowing it, Dr. Selye presented the world with an excellent argument for living the yogic lifestyle—a life of moderation—when he found that a life with greater and more intense demands for adaptation would tend to be shorter than the life moderately lived.

Intense demands for adaptation stress the body, and this creates "underbreathing," a shallow and sometimes rapid breathing pattern that is frequently outside of our awareness. We may notice only that we feel a mild sense of anxiety and/or fatigue or that things just don't feel right. But this stressed, shallow breathing stresses the body further and, in turn, creates more underbreathing. This self-perpetuating cycle, called a positive feedback loop, has become almost epidemic in our society today.

The yogic techniques of *pranayama*, the practice of controlled breathing patterns, break the underbreathing cycle and restore our bodies and minds to their natural calm. We then have more energy, which in yoga is called *prana*, or the life force.

Creating Change: Easy Pranayama

To become familiar with the stresses in your life and the adaptation you must make to cope with them, try the following breathing technique. Sit down, relax, and breathe slowly and deeply. Use this pranayama technique to clear your mind and come into the present. Try it for 5–10 minutes to begin. Breathe in for a count of eight, hold for four counts, and then breathe out for a count of eight. Each count should take about one second, so you can use the standard one-thousand-one, one-thousand-two, one-thousand-three, etc. Some yogis like to count using the word *Om: Om*-one, *Om*-two, *Om*-three, etc.

When you feel relaxed and more "present," think about the stress you now have in your life. Think of how you have had to adapt. Consider what else you will have to do either to fully adapt or come to terms with the stress. Make a list of the things that stress you, and write down the feelings and thoughts associated with them. Don't worry about neatness. Let your writing follow your stream of consciousness, and let it flow. As you write, think about and feel the stress subsiding and melting away.

When you have finished writing, close your eyes and reflect on the following scenario. Imagine how you will feel about this stress ten years from now. See yourself looking back on the situation a decade in the future. Feel the distance you now have from those feelings, and use this future perspective to reduce the effect the stress has on you now. Remember the old saying, "Distance lends enchantment to the view."

Non-violence and Health

One of the basic tenets of yoga is the practice of *ahimsa* (non-violence). We already know that we should not be violent toward others, but the yoga masters tell us that the real need is to become non-violent within ourselves—in all of our thoughts and feelings. Only when we achieve a continuous state of this non-violence, they say, will we stop creating the harmful effects of violence.

Modern experts have found that our thoughts and emotions are like waves of messages washing over all of the cells of the body and that destructive mental images, thoughts, or feelings affect our health and sense of well-being. It is well-documented that these messages can affect our health by enlivening or suppressing the immune system, that the immune system's ability to ward off illness is weakened by negative emotions like anger and despair, that forgiveness has a healing effect on the mind and body, that becoming a more forgiving person insures better health by reducing stress, and that the failure to forgive, and blaming others, are related to cardiovascular diseases and cancer.

We tend to get caught up in negative thinking, the experts say, when we rehash the details of a past traumatic event. When we repeatedly go over how things "could have happened" or "should have been," we invoke the emotions connected with that experience and relive them. Then, fueled by these feelings, we become more anxious, depressed, angry, or agitated. We may even lose the ability to escape these feelings and become lodged in "shoulds" or "coulds."

To forgive the past and move into positive thoughts and feelings, we have to let go of how we wanted things to turn out. When "how things should be" becomes the focus in our lives, we miss the pleasure of this moment and may even lose sight of the fact that there is more in our lives than anger, loss, or hurt. When we are caught up in negative mental dialogue, our ability to feel love, pleasure, or beauty is either diminished or eliminated.

> To accept reality as it is, we have to give up expecting or wanting things from other people that they cannot or will not give us.

So how do we return to positive feelings? By changing the way we think and feel! Try the following technique to replace negative thoughts or feelings with positive ones, and give the mind/body better health.

Creating Change: Gratitude List

Making a "gratitude list" can open the door a crack to a more positive life view and balance your perspective. Every time you are stuck in negative thinking, stop and make a list of positive things, people, or experiences that

you are grateful for. You may not actually feel the gratitude right now, but you know that the gratitude exists,
and you are reminding your unconscious mind of it as
you make the list. When you are trapped in negativity or
distress, make at least one list every day (make it just
before bedtime so you can sleep on it). In time you will
transform the negative into positive.

It's Not Personal

External events may keep us from feeling happy, and
when this happens it is important to remember that deper-
sonalizing a situation can be helpful. Let's imagine that we
feel unhappy, angry, frustrated, overpowered, or hurt
because we have had a fight with our son, mother, daughter, father, or lover. Or imagine that the boss insulted us in
front of the entire office staff and then took credit for our
work. No matter what the scenario, their behavior was
wrong, hurtful, thoughtless, and maybe even mean. At first
we're outraged. We think, "How could they do that?" We
don't feel respected or valued. It hurts. What should we do?
Just be upset for a while and then bury it? No. Remember
that things tend to come back and haunt us when we try to
repress them. Instead of ignoring the event, we can try
looking at the situation from another point of view.

When we can see that what happened was not necessarily personal, the other person's actions will feel less
hurtful. Often these people are simply reflecting their
own unconscious issues (past pains, expectations, or

grievances), and they are usually not aware that they are projecting their own issues outside themselves and blaming others for their own shortcomings. As long as they can assign the fault to someone else, they escape their own blame, shame, and pain, and so they distance themselves from the event that created it. (Often, when people say "you," they are unknowingly talking about themselves.) We need to step back and see the other person's lack of awareness, see their desperation, and how their "need to be right," negative training, or lack of maturity creates their behavior. We need to step back and see that the problem really belongs to them and has little to do with us. When we can do that, the situation becomes less personal and much less painful. By widening our perspective in this way, we become more objective.

Understanding the other person's behavior can help us open our minds and hearts to a larger picture of reality and relationships. And this understanding can ease our negative thinking and stop us from taking things too personally.

> As we gain life experience, our beliefs, commitments, and opinions change.

Creating Change: Widening Your Perspective

To practice widening your perspective, try reflecting on the offenders' suffering. They may have acted out of fear or pain and may not have been able to help themselves. For example, the boss who belittles people may be doing so because he feels inept and anxious about his job. Perhaps he was belittled in childhood and is acting out as a product of his upbringing. Debilitated by his own insecurity and desperate to gain some feeling of self-worth, perhaps he is lying in order to relieve his misery.

If we can see that those who offended us were trying to escape their own misery, we can also see that their actions aren't personal. They would have done the same thing to anyone standing in our position at that time. This doesn't make their actions right or OK, but it will make them understandable and less personal—and therefore less painful.

Killing Relationships

The people who love us want us to be involved in their lives, and they want to be involved in ours. If we are obsessing over a past conflict or loss, we may not be giving them the attention they need. With our focus trained on pain, anger, or loss, those closest to us may be feeling left out, ignored, or just unimportant to us. They may be hurt because they think our suffering is more important to us than they are. Obsessive anger or grief, coupled with lack of attention to those who are close to us, takes its toll on even the closest relationships.

What is more, it is difficult for those who love us to keep watching us struggle and suffer when there is nothing they can do to help us. Or they may be strongly affected by our feelings and take on our negativity as if it were their own.

We all know how infectious a bad mood can be; even casual acquaintances are affected by our negative or depressed energy. After a while, they may begin to avoid our company, and over time, even our closest relationships may be jeopardized because of the pull of our negative thoughts and feelings. By changing our words or feelings, even if only for a few minutes, we can soften the impact of our negative energy—both for ourselves and for those around us.

Creating Change: Changing Our Feelings

When we speak or write positively, we change the waves of messages our body is receiving from negative into positive. And even a few minutes of thinking positively can change the effect we have on others as well as on our own health and well-being. Try the following technique to gain some positive focus.

Take a break from negativity by choosing to think and speak in a positive way. Tell someone you care about how much he or she means to you. Go into detail about the specific behaviors you admire and respect. Or write letters to friends to let them know just how important they are to your life—even if you don't elect to mail them all. Do it right away and do it often—at least once a day.

How Long? It's Eating Up Life!

How long are we going to live? How many days, months, or years do we have left on this earth? How much of that time do we want to devote to emotions like hurt, anger, or resentment? How much do we want to blame and complain? Would we still be concerned with our boss's words or what our parent didn't give us if we had only one week left to live? Probably not.

We would probably choose to think about the best experiences we could, because our time would be too valuable to waste on anything negative. And since we do not know when our last moments will be, maybe we should consider choosing the best life experience as a regular practice. We have this choice every second we are alive.

We can choose to release the negative and embrace the positive. We begin by making the decision to do it. This is often the easy part, for after the decision is made, we have to follow through. This can be more difficult because it involves letting go of the past and the familiar—and staying vigilant to the constant positive choices we need to make.

Creating Change: Choose and Follow Through

Make a decision and follow through. Start with something small. For example, decide to sing a song every time you take a shower or when you get up the first thing in the morning. Decide to do this for a specific time period like a week or a month. Make sure that you choose something you can definitely do, then promise yourself that you will stick with it, no matter what happens. Then follow through. After you have been successful the first time, make several more similar decisions. These small victories are a great preparation for following through on more difficult decisions like choosing to embrace the positive.

chapter three

UNDERSTANDING

PATANJALI'S *YOGA SUTRA,* the earliest and most comprehensive text on yoga, describes several ways in which the mind can perceive the world. Among them are *pramana* (correct perception), *viparyaya* (incorrect perception), and *vikalpa* (imagination).

Pramana, or correct perception, can also be defined as comprehension, clear understanding, or knowing that something is true. There are three levels of correct perception: direct perception, or experience; indirect perception, which involves some experience; and inference, which relies on another's experience.

> *Direct Perception:* If a car crashed into your living room while you were sitting there watching TV, your knowledge would be directly perceived. There would be no doubt because the accident would be your direct experience.

Indirect Perception: If you were upstairs in the bedroom and someone came to tell you of the crash after you had felt the house shake and heard the sounds, you would know it was true through indirect perception.

Inference: If someone you knew and trusted called you when you were at work and said a car had crashed into your living room, you would know by inference that it was true. Or if, years later, the crash was recorded in an official document, others could know it was true—also by inference.

Viparyaya is incorrect perception. If a recording of a car crashing into a house were played while you were in the garage, you might have thought that the car had actually crashed into your living room.

Vikalpa is imagination. If you had lived in fear (vikalpa, with an emotional component) that a car would come careening into your house some day because you lived on a busy corner, you might have been convinced by almost any loud noise in the street that this had actually taken place. Vipararyaya (incorrect perception) plus vikalpa (imagination) may create a believable reality that never really happens.

Understanding the Situation

On our journey to forgive, it is important to objectively understand how an unresolved conflict arose, how we functioned in it, why we behaved as we did, and how things are right now. It is also important to understand how we feel about what happened. We need clarity so we can move on.

In order to get an accurate reading of current discord, we need to go over the triggering event systematically, paying close attention to our feelings—not only immediately accessible feelings, but also the deeper, underlying feelings. Writing in a journal regularly can help us both discover and express how we feel, and it can also reduce our emotional stress while we take note of the lessons we learn.

Journaling can also help us understand the conflict from other perspectives. So spend some time thinking about what happened and the way everyone involved behaved. Tell the story only to those who have no investment in the situation and can be objective. Listen to their response as if it were information only. Since what they say may not be correct or valid, listen without personalizing it. (There is time to do that later, after some "alone-time" reflection.) If they have given you unbiased insights and opinions, their feedback may be helpful. (And sometimes we are able to gain information from just imagining how another might describe what happened.)

Creating Change: Imagine Another Perspective

Try to imagine how someone who knows you would describe your stressful situation as well as the behavior of all the people involved—including yours. You can often gain new insight, lessons, and information by creating a mental image of how a mother, brother, uncle, or trusted friend would talk about it. Just sit quietly for a while. Imagine you are that person and then describe the situation, either in your mind or in your journal. Be objective when you think about what they would say.

We Are Not Alone

It can seem as if our trouble is unique and unusual, but actually there are many people out there who feel the same way we do right now. Knowing that conflict is common to everyone does not take the pain away, of course, but it may help us feel better to know that we are not alone. It can be comforting to recognize that others are experiencing the same feelings and struggles that we are. For example, studies indicate that right now more than fifteen percent of American parents and their children (about 45 million people) are not speaking to each other. That means that millions are contending with the same issue at the same time. Many have already survived their struggles with issues much like ours—and we too will survive. We may need to learn more about ourselves or make a few healthy changes, but we can and will make it.

The Whole Perspective: The Story of Cinderella

We all know the story of Cinderella, the poor, brave, beautiful girl whose beloved father died, leaving everything to his greedy wife. She and her two mean daughters treated Cinderella terribly, filling her life with drudgery, fear, pain, and sorrow. Cinderella's best friends were mice, for goodness sake! Thankfully, her godmother's intervention saved the day for our heroine. She married a handsome prince, became a princess, and lived in luxury surrounded by loving people.

This is how Cinderella's story is told, but what about the other people in this tale? Is this the story they would tell or would their version of it be different? Take a minute to imagine how this story would be told by one of the other characters. The following is an example of just one possibility for "The Stepmother's Story:"

I married this nice, slightly dim, and inept man. We had different values, so it was a difficult marriage, but he was sweet. It turned out to be a short union, however—he died after only a few months. His last testament left everything to me, so my daughters and I were financially secure. But his death also left me saddled with the care of his lazy, sneaky daughter, Cinderella. After his demise, she became impossible to handle.

Cinderella didn't obey or even respond to the simplest requests. She sulked and skulked around the house into all hours of the night, talking to mice. It was a trying situation, and it became even worse when my daughters

received an invitation to the prince's ball.
Cinderella really began to sneak around then,
stealing clothing from my girls and shirking
her household responsibilities. She said she
was going to the ball no matter what, even if
she was not invited.

In Cinderella's normal, manipulative style,
she crashed the ball, monopolized all of the
prince's time, and wrecked my daughters'
chances to win his favor. I was told she
found some old gypsy woman to help her
and bribed her with money she stole—probably from us. The whole thing was humili-
ating and very disappointing. Were one of
my girls to wed the prince, we would finally attain our proper station in life, but Cindy,
thinking only of herself as usual, ruined our
chances just for her own selfish gain.

This version of the stepmother's story is very different
from the original tale in which Cinderella is the heroine.
Faced with both stories, which would the stepmother say
was the correct version? Her own, of course! Each person
will always believe that his or her perspective is the real
one, the right one (and maybe even the only one). So if
everyone believes his or her own version of a situation,
which one is right? It all depends on which of the many
possible viewpoints we have access to. Blind men who

stand at different places around an elephant will describe that elephant differently because they have access only to a part of the whole; people who experience only their own perceptions rarely know the entire story.

Expecting that other people will accept our perspective over theirs is, most often, naïve. But when we can understand and accept the fact that different people see a difficult situation differently, and that no one view is the "right" one, we are free to choose our own responses.

Creating Change: Another Cinderella Story

Take a few minutes to imagine the Cinderella story from the perspective of one of the other people in it—a stepdaughter, the stepmother, the king, the queen, or the prince. Write this story down as "The King's Tale," "The Stepdaughter's Story," or "The Prince's Story," and remember to tell it from the perspective of their fears, wishes, weaknesses, dreams, and needs. After writing down these stories in detail, can you begin to see how everyone would believe his or her own position was just as valid as any other?

> Life is an ever-changing event that we experience from an ever-changing perspective.

Life Is an Ongoing Hypothesis

The *Yoga Sutra* tells us that our mental processes produce thoughts that are ultimately either painful or painless. This is borne out by the fact that as we remember an experience, we highlight specific parts of it in our own minds, according to what we liked or disliked. And this (usually unconscious) underscoring of our preferences creates the focus for the way we describe a situation and the story we tell about it. Then, as we focus on the highlighted details, we minimize the others until, over time, they are forgotten. Our memories are influenced by whether an experience is good, mediocre, or bad.

In other words, our bias shrinks our memory and distorts our perspective. And further, when there are others who experienced the same event along with us, we create an even stronger lock onto our partial version of the event as we talk among ourselves. When we describe and replay the highlights in our minds, we cement them into our view of history.

Sharon Cottor, an extraordinary therapist in Scottsdale, Arizona has said, "The past is yet to be determined." Some interesting and telling research studies demonstrate her point, showing that memories change over time and are usually only partial reconstructions of an actual event. Even though our memories seem vividly accurate to us, in reality they are skewed by the way we describe an event to others and ourselves.

In one well-monitored research study, a large group of people was exposed to the same experience. In discussions held with the whole group, everyone agreed on exactly what had happened. They all shared the same vision of the experience. Then the subjects were separated into subgroups that met periodically to discuss what they remembered of the experience. The subgroups had no contact with one another.

All of the stories had changed by the end of the study. When the entire group was brought back together, they no longer agreed. The original memory that all the subjects had shared had changed. The members of each subgroup were in agreement with the other members of their own group, but all of the groups had different collective memories.

The memory of the original experience had changed over time and through interaction. According to Sharon Cottor, "This happens to all of us whether we are aware of it or not. For instance, our childhood memories are always selective and inac-

> When we experience the same event along with others, and we talk among ourselves about what happened, we create a strong lock onto a partial version of the memory. We describe and replay the highlights in our minds and cement them in our collective view of history.

curate. People remember some things that did not happen. They emphasize some parts of their story while diminishing others. This editing relates more to their current life experiences and circumstances than to the past event itself. No matter what version we select (or remember) to tell of the past, there is always more past to tell."

Letting Go

Everyone and everything changes over time; in fact, change is the only constant in life. Every moment is a new beginning when we let go of the "familiar" past, but we act as if people and situations are static. We know that we have changed through our own experiences, but we talk and act as if other people have remained the same.

Remembering that people may be different from the way they were when past conflicts arose will help us let go of the old stereotype we have assigned to them and improve our relationships. As long as we remember that change is constant, we will be able to remain open and meet these people with new eyes. It is our outdated prejudices that do not allow us to see them as they are now. And repeatedly thinking of someone in negative terms can easily become a habit. It may be comfortable to dwell in old mental grooves, but this comfort comes at a price. On the other hand, if we can eliminate our old prejudices, we foster good relationships.

Negative Thoughts

Our minds create negative thoughts. They are not who we are. Sometimes negative thinking and behavior is learned from other people, but more often it is the result of feelings that are born from negative experiences. (Thinking and behavior are also influenced by what we eat and drink, how we exercise, how much stress we are under, and the choices we make.)

Negative feelings can be changed. Through investigation and reframing, negative thoughts and feelings can be turned into positive ones. But to make these changes, we first need to know what our thoughts and feelings really are.

At a seminar on money, Todd learned that his unconscious thinking had determined his attitude toward money. He started paying more attention to this "background thinking" and was surprised to find that his mind was repeating several negative phrases about money. "I'm poor," "I can't afford that," and "People who have money are bad," he would think. After Todd discovered that he had done this unconscious programming in his mind, he explored some pivotal money moments of his life and found the ideas and decisions that had created his unconscious feelings. He began working to transform his negativity—and in a short time he did.

Todd realized that he had been taught by his parents that money created bad people, and as a child he had decided he did not want to have money. He wanted to remain a good person. After he discovered how he had programmed his mind, Todd's thinking changed, as did his feelings about money—and consequently, his life. He was no longer trapped into behaving in specific ways because of his unconscious background thinking. We can transform ourselves, too.

Creating Change: Background Thinking

The following technique can help you become more aware of your background thinking. First, pick a subject that brings up negative thoughts (or one that you want to change). Relax, and let your mind wander around this subject while you remain aware of what it is saying. Write down any new thoughts you find there that you would like to change. Then, as you go about your day, stay on the lookout for these newly-discovered negative thoughts—and whenever possible replace them with positive ones. Each time the negative thought returns, change it. It will take repeated practice, but the rewards for your effort are great.

chapter four

ATTACHMENT AND EXPECTATIONS

THE SANSKRIT WORD *KLESHA* COMES from the root *klish,* meaning "to inflict" [pain]. According to the ancient yoga masters, attachment, *raga,* is one of the five kleshas. (The others are ignorance, *avidya;* ego, *asmita;* aversion, *devesha;* and fear, *abhinivesha.*) The kleshas are all submerged in our consciousness, the ancients say, like icebergs—only a small part of each is ever clearly in view. But they are the root cause of all unhappiness.

Because attachment is one of the kleshas, the yoga masters taught the importance of releasing our ties to past and future desired results (and things), as well as to an excessive connection to our self-image. Letting go of our attachments (or reaching a state of what they called non-attachment) is a prerequisite for forgiveness.

In yoga, detaching does not mean that we become cool or wooden. On the contrary, relinquishing our hurtful attachments gives us the freedom to live a life that is not restricted by unresolved painful experiences. When we can forgive and let go of our attachments to specific outcomes, past painful incidents, and the hurtful behavior of others, we will be able to experience the present moment more intensely—and this is where we find abiding happiness.

Attachment

Attachment is an emotional bonding to people, places, ideas, and things. We can become attached to almost anything—shoes, pets, football teams, equipment, or a favorite seat in a classroom, to name a few. We can feel an emotional bonding with sounds, sights, stores, clothing, food (ask any chocolate lover), or the effects of words and actions. Attachments may bring temporary pleasure, but they can also cause pain and suffering.

Attachments can bind us to discomfort, restrict our options, and obfuscate our perspective—and losing what we are attached to can create great upset and hurt. For instance, when we are attached to a relationship that has been dissolved, we feel the pain of separation. This is natural. It lasts for a time and is over. But when we resist accepting the loss of that relationship, the pain does not stop—it continues long past the natural grieving time. In fact, it persists for as long as we insist that the situation be different from the way it is.

Any time we allow our happiness, peace of mind, or sense of being loved, to be dependent upon our attachments, we abandon our ability to remain in the present moment—and that's the only place we can experience abiding happiness. Letting go of our attachments and accepting reality as it is, the yogis say, is the key to freedom. Remaining content with the reality at hand and fully experiencing each moment of life are the ingredients for an easy, satisfying, and happy life. To move in this direction, we need to learn more about our attachments.

> The ancient yoga masters tell us that only when we release ourselves from attachment and remain content with the present moment, can we be truly happy.

Creating Change: Investigating Attachments

Keep an Attachment Journal. Each time an angry or hurtful thought comes to mind, sit down, be still, and take ten consecutive slow and deep breaths. Lengthen each inhalation and exhalation. Then sit quietly and reflect on the situation and the attachment that generated your negative emotions. Write about the What, Who, and Why of each of the attachments you discover. Also consider the origin of each attachment and how it works in your life. Another way to keep your Attachment Journal is to thoroughly examine one attachment each day while sitting for 10–20 minutes in a meditative posture.

Expectations

Expectations are a form of attachment. They are learned from parents, created or shaped by the experiences of life, or modeled after the behavior of others—and they make our lives and relationships difficult. In fact, they are humanity's main reason for struggle, turmoil, and unhappiness. Feelings of anger, frustration, anxiety, resentment, and hurt result from unmet expectations. Lillian Dangott, Ph.D., an extraordinary psychotherapist in Verdi, Nevada, explains how expectations are hard on relationships:

> People believe that what they expect from others is universal, but expectations are not universal. They are subjective. No matter how real the expectations may feel or how many people have validated them, expectations are still subjective. Expectations are a setup for disappointment.
>
> It's hard to see our own expectations and how they affect others. The challenge is to have our expectations be as few as possible, as non-specific as possible, and as low as possible. Otherwise we become unhappy, demanding, needy, and disappointed—all of which burden friendships, as well as ourselves.
>
> Maybe the worst part of having high expectations is that they are a setup for disappointment and depression. We can be

very forgiving and understanding of where
we are coming from, but we don't tend to be
that way with others. When our expectations
aren't met, the disappointment and hurt we
feel doesn't allow us to see the love, though
imperfect, that others are trying to give us.
This is one way our expectations foster a
negative life view.

When we insist that our way is "the right way," anyone
who does not live up to our ideas will fall short of our
expectations and leave us disappointed, irritated, frustrated, hurt, fearful, or angry. Then, when we tell our friends
and family about a "wrong" we suffered, they validate our
"right" position, and this makes us feel better. It validates
our point of view and reinforces our idea that everyone
shares the same expectations. So if we want to be able to
let go and forgive, it is important to remember that expectations are subjective—not universal.

All people do not share the same expectations. We
each have our own preconceived ideas of how others
should behave, talk, and live. Often we don't even realize
that we have them. Some of our expectations are outdated and no longer true. Karen's therapist gave her a good
example of this.

Karen thought that if her lover really loved
her, he would know what to say and do to

make her happy. When he told her he didn't, she didn't believe him. She remained skeptical even after their therapist told her the same thing. Why? The therapist suggested the following possibility: when Karen was a small child, she felt unloved. Her father was dead, and her mother rarely bothered to figure out what Karen needed. Obsessed with her own pain, she left Karen unnoticed and feeling unloved, and the emotional deprivation in her childhood became an unconscious part of her expectations. Without realizing it, Karen still believed that if people truly loved her, they would figure out what she needed and wanted.

Whenever our expectations about the way others "should" think or treat us, or how our lives "should be" are not met, negative feelings and distorted ideas arise. This happens around all unmet expectations, whether they are ours or someone else's. Here are a few examples of common expectations:

- *I should be rewarded and treated better.* Absolutely! But continuing to expect something that is not happening, and feeling disappointed every time the "deserved" treatment isn't there, doesn't make a happy life. Let it go!
- *My children should give me more attention.* They

should! But if they won't or can't, stop expecting it! Right now they may not be the people you think they are (or would like them to be). Let it go!

- *They shouldn't act that way.* Remember, while that may be true from our perspective, it may not be true from theirs. Stop setting yourself up for disappointment. Let it go!

- *They should have known better—been more considerate.* Absolutely! But that is not who they were at the time. Maybe they did know better or maybe they didn't. Remember, everyone makes mistakes. The mistake that is happening right now is the disappointment and hurt we are experiencing from our own expectations. Let them go!

- *They owe me an apology.* They probably do! But maybe they can't admit they were wrong or are just too afraid to apologize. That is their problem. We don't need to make it our problem. Time to let it go and move on.

We are always going to suffer when we expect things that we don't have the power to make happen. In order to feel better, we must stop hurting ourselves because other people cannot or will not conform to our expectations. When we can change these expectations into wishes, we can live easier, happier lives. The following exercise can help us get to know what our unrealistic expectations are.

Creating Change: Uncovering Expectations

Make a list of all the expectations you have about a situation that has been causing you pain. Write your expectations down. Go over each of them, one at a time, exploring where it came from, how it serves you, how it harms your relationships, and why you might not want to keep it. In your mind's eye, envision the same situation without that expectation. Finally, rewrite that expectation down as a hope or wish.

Empty Rules

Unrealistic expectations lead us to think people should behave in particular ways, and that these "shoulds" are invisible "rules" to be followed in order for us to know our expectations are being met. But unless we have examined our expectations very carefully, we are probably not aware of the rules associated with them.

For example, if one of our rules is, "They should be grateful," you are right. But how does that gratefulness look? What is it they needed to have said or done that would have made their behavior seem grateful? We may think, "If they really cared, they would have brought flowers or said the dinner was great." This would prove to us that our expectation that they should be grateful is being met. But often we are unaware of this dynamic. All we may know is that someone is not behaving the way we think they should and we feel powerless to change him or her.

The rules surrounding our expectations are empty. If

there were an instruction booklet on how we should behave, and an agreement that everyone would perform accordingly, then the rules that give proof to our expectations might be serviceable. But when others do not know or care about the rules and do not follow them, we feel that we have been wronged and seek others for comfort and support.

Unfortunately, however, it doesn't matter how many people agree with us or how strong their support is. Our own rules are still not binding. And even though the approval of our friends and family may feel good temporarily, in the long run their support works against our healing because it clouds our perceptions, entrenches us in a polarized position, and solidifies our belief in our own "rightness."

For example, when I was about to walk into a courtroom, because a crooked storage company manager had stolen everything I owned (before he declared bankruptcy and died), my attorney turned to me and said, "When you are being cross-examined, remember to ask yourself whether you would rather be 'right' or win this case." He was concerned that if I fixated on being right, I would end up expressing the outrage and huge upset that I felt as I told the courtroom what had been done to me. My attorney was right—I would have really let them know how bad it was. My attorney believed that my need to be right, as I told the court how wrong the offender was, would be used by the defendant's highly paid corporate attorneys to negatively influence the jury against me. So I held my tongue and my emotions—and proved his wise advice.

Believing we are right will not relieve our pain—remember that our pain comes from attachment to a pleasurable event that has taken place in the past. The best way to find present and future happiness is to learn to identify the rules that are attached to our expectations so that we can modify them. The following technique can help us discover them.

Creating Change: Identifying the Rules

Each day write down one of your expectations. Look for the words "should" or "must" that are associated with it. Wherever you find these words, you will be able to find an unrealistic expectation. Spend meditative time contemplating it. Make a list of the unenforceable rules attached to this expectation and ask yourself what kind of behavior would tell you that the other people involved are behaving properly. Simply becoming aware of the "rules" that surround an expectation will soften their effect. Rewrite the expectation without any rules—reframe it as a hope or wish.

Our expectations can become our jailers.

The Formula: R ± E = ±S

This simple formula, from Sharon Cottor, is the key to living a pleasant life. The formula is, "Reality plus or minus Expectations equals positive or negative Satisfaction." When our expectations are greater than the reality of the

situation, we are disappointed, dissatisfied, or unhappy
(R − E = −S). Satisfaction grows as expectations diminish.
When our expectations of a situation (reality) are low and
the reality exceeds them (R − E = +S), we feel good.

> When her dad came into town, Sue was
> expecting him to buy her a new skirt to wear
> to an upcoming party. When he took her
> shopping for an entire outfit—from under-
> wear to hat—she was delighted. What her
> dad did (the reality) was greater than Sue's
> expectations of what he would do, so Sue
> was very satisfied (R − E = +S).

If we reverse Sue's experience, it's easy to see that she
would have been disappointed if her father had not
bought her a new skirt as she expected. By the same
token, if Sue were able to expect little or nothing in all of
her relationships, she would feel satisfied more of the
time. If she could remember the formula and identify her
expectations, she could avert future disappointment. With
this simple formula, maybe we can, too.

Creating Change: R ± E = ±S

Every time you are disappointed, try using this formula to identify the expectation that caused it. Write it
down. Imagine lowering or eliminating your expectations in that situation. Write a paragraph on how the

same situation would look, feel, and play out if you had little or no expectations. Notice that by reducing or eliminating your expectations, you open yourself to a more positive experience.

Guilt: Forgiving Ourselves

Guilt is a huge subject, but for our purpose we can say that guilt is associated with how we need to see ourselves in order to feel good about who we are. As it relates to the "shoulds," guilt is a form of expectation born out of attachment. It is the result of our behaving in ways we know are wrong or not meeting an expectation we have set for ourselves.

Guilt can be productive when it protects us from our own excesses. If we feel guilty about something we have done or failed to do, we can apologize, make amends, learn from our mistakes, and decide to change our behavior because of it. But some guilt requires a deeper look.

Jim was standing in line at the car rental counter right behind an antsy guy who couldn't get to the counter fast enough. When the antsy guy left to go further down the counter to wait in front of another representative, the clerk called, "Next." Since the man was gone and would be served where he was, Jim stepped forward to rent his car. But as he was leaving the antsy guy barked at him, telling him he shouldn't have taken his place in line. Jim was irritated and retorted that he saw that the antsy guy was about to be served. But after his irritation had worn off, Jim felt a little guilty. He didn't think that he had done anything wrong, but he couldn't shake the slight gnawing feeling of guilt.

The antsy guy had touched a nerve; but what that nerve was, Jim wasn't sure, so he spent some time clearing his mind. And when he got some objective feedback, he realized that the antsy guy's words had brought to light some guilty feelings about what Jim expected from himself.

Jim felt guilty because his actions did not jibe with his self-image. Once he examined the situation and his part in it, however, he realized that he had been influenced by messages delivered to him with anger, and that he didn't have to accept the guilt assigned to him by someone else. He saw that the guilt he felt came from a discrepancy between his self-image and his actual actions. If the antsy guy hadn't said anything, Jim might not have become aware of his feelings. Jim also felt shame and embarrassment (feelings that frequently accompany guilt), because he thought other people might disapprove of his actions.

His own image and what others thought of him were important to Jim, and when he looked deep into himself, he found that he really did believe that the antsy guy should have had gone first. His "guilt nerve" had been struck because he had not acted in accordance with the way he would like to see himself (his standards).

It is important that we know what we believe is appropriate behavior, the standards we have set for ourselves, and our boundaries. Try this investigative technique to take a closer look at what can trigger guilty feelings. Then let go of them. Forgiving ourselves is as important as forgiving others.

Creating Change: Forgiving Ourselves

With your journal at hand, think of a situation that made you feel guilty. In your mind's eye, review the experience. Remember the location, surroundings, smells, thoughts, temperature, etc., in detail. As you replay the scene, look closely for moments when you felt confusion or hesitation. For now, ignore the reasons your mind may give you to justify those feelings. Write down what you did or said that you would change if you could. Write down the ideas you have about your ideal behavior in this type of situation. Write down the way your behavior differed from this ideal, and remember—we are all human. If circumstances had been different, you would have behaved differently. Ask yourself if you did the best you could have under the circumstances at that moment. Then let it go!

chapter five

THE VICTIM-VICTIMIZER STORY

YOGA PHILOSOPHY TELLS US THAT the regular practice of *svadhyaya* (self-study) is one of the building blocks for living a happy life. Reflecting on our own nature, it says, and exploring how we function, think, and feel is critical to our ability to experience happiness as well as to forgive.

We may think we know ourselves, but that is often not the case. What are we really doing? As life changes, so do we, and as we change we may not always update our outdated decisions, ideas, and feelings. This leaves us stuck with obsolete information and habits that no longer apply to our lives. Unless we pay attention to ourselves (to discover the many layers of our being and reevaluate new changes we have made), we continue to function according to outmoded ideas and feelings.

Our Stories

When we are talking about something that happened, whether describing our vacation or telling the story of our life, we include only a few of the millions of moments that actually took place. It would be impossibly time-consuming and unimaginably boring to describe every moment. Imagine giving a detailed description of every second we sit in a car or wait in line. And since we cannot include everything, we must select and share just a few moments—enough to give the flavor of our experience and the spirit of our message.

We share these moments in the same way we would share photos of a trip. We describe a series of mental pictures that evoke the event and we add some commentary made up of our opinions, feelings, and interpretations. We talk about all of the events in our lives through this same filter—this is how our stories are made.

Sometimes we tell our stories to help organize our thoughts or understand ourselves better. Sometimes we tell our stories so others will understand how we became the way we are. Faced with a situation that requires forgiveness, our hurt feelings will naturally drive us to tell the story in a way that will highlight our unjust treatment and the wrongness of the offender (or the situation). This can help us feel better momentarily by garnering sympathy and validation, but rarely is it an accurate or objective account of what actually happened. It has been filtered by our current feelings and ideas.

For example, we might describe a friend's behavior as "direct or assertive" while we describe an enemy's same behavior as "rude and aggressive." Same behavior, different description—it just depends on what we think and feel about the person we're talking about. As our feelings and thoughts change, the story will change, too.

The Victim-Victimizer Story

What we tell and how we tell it may also be determined by how we want others to perceive us. Our manner and style of delivery, as well as the information we highlight, colors our story and greatly influences the listener's thoughts and feelings. If we need support or want to gain sympathy and validation, we need only to tell our story in the "right" way to damage the offender's reputation. Sympathetic listeners will reinforce our position—our "rightness"—with their compassion and agreement. We feel temporarily better as a result of this venting and validation, and this makes us inclined to tell our story again and again. When we present ourselves as the injured party and someone else as the villain, our story is a victim-victimizer (VV) story. It may help us momentarily manage some of the pain we are feeling, but it is an obstacle on our path to forgiveness.

Rerunning our victim-victimizer story prevents (or at least slows down) our ability to let go, move into the present moment, and experience happiness. The support and compassion our story elicits keeps us from letting go of the disturbing event. But our objective is to be free of negative thoughts and feelings, not to cement ourselves into them. And to be free, we have to let go of the grievance. This does not mean we have to condone or accept bad behavior. Let's begin to create change by exploring how our feelings color our words and thus the thoughts of others.

Creating Change: Changing Feelings— Changing Thoughts

Write a short description of how someone you like behaves. When you have finished, imagine that person has now done something awful and you are angry with him or her. Now write another description of that person's same behavior. Notice that just changing your feelings changed the story you tell. Use your journal to jot down what you learn.

What Do We Get from Telling the VV Story?

Being a victim may not feel good, but it has its benefits, its "upside." Here are a few examples:

- Victims can take guilt and responsibility from themselves and place it all on the offender.
- Victims can receive extra sympathy, tenderness, caring, courtesy, and consideration. They get their way—and a lot of attention.
- Holding a grudge can give victims a subtle sense of superiority over others. They can think they are special in some way.

But there comes a point at which venting re-creates the event. Research has shown that repeatedly telling our VV story renews the same negative feelings that arose when the grievance took place. And these feelings, which would normally fade and disappear, are fed and kept strong as we repeatedly relive them.

It's especially difficult to stop telling our VV story when a relationship has been dissolved. Hanging on to it through retelling our story may help us keep the lost relationship alive in our minds, but it can also exacerbate our hurt feelings and fan our strengthening anger. This can help us feel stronger and more stable momentarily, for anger temporarily blots out our feelings of insecurity, hurt, and fear. Anger can also give us a momentary sense of superiority. But revisiting anger in this way is risky for our health and happiness. The feelings of strength, stability, and superiority we gain are simply an illusion. They can only mask our hurt for a short time.

> Letting go of our victim-victimizer story, forgiving, and moving on with our lives is the only way to truly release our emotional pain.

As long as we continue to tell our victim-victimizer story, either in our own minds or to others, we will not be able to forgive. We have to stop telling it, no matter how justified it seems or how much validation we get from it. Letting go of the story, forgiving the offender, and moving on with our lives is the only way to find true release from painful emotions and thoughts. VV stories keep us locked into a polarized point of view that eliminates any possibility of change or growth.

Creating Change: Stop It!

One way to help us stop telling our victim-victimizer story is to just say, "Stop it!" The following technique may be helpful. When a bad situation has upset you and you feel angry, limit telling your story to two or three times. When you do tell it, get into all the details—be thorough, and after the second time make a decision to stop. The next time you feel like telling the story, make it your absolute last time. Don't allow yourself to repeat it again. Don't even let yourself replay it in your mind. Each time you feel that you need or want to retell the story, stop. Instead, take a few moments to breathe deeply and slowly. Sit down (or lie down) and consciously breathe for ten to twenty long breaths. Then drink a large glass of water and take a walk. If you still need to tell your VV story, then sit down and write it out.

Write down every detail of what happened and how you think and feel about it. Don't worry about the way the writing looks—just keep writing until you feel completely done. Begin and end your writing with the following sentences: "I am on a healing journey. As I write my story, the pain and suffering move from inside me out onto the paper, freeing my mind and heart."

Fear Can Be an Obstacle

The victim-victimizer story can take many forms, and one of the most subtle has to do with fear. Fear is a natural part of living. We all experience it, and it is occasionally helpful. But fear is neither helpful nor healthy when it subdues desire, prevents free action, or stresses life. Under these conditions, we have become fear's victim. Fear has become a life-limiting obstacle.

There are many things people fear besides the obvious ones that have to do with death and disaster. Ernest Becker, in his Pulitzer Prize–winning book, *The Denial of Death,* also talks about the many small fears that arise daily, such as making mistakes, embarrassing ourselves, or feeling foolish.

Fear is a very real part of every human life, and we need to accept the possibility that it will sometimes be a part of our experience. We need a way to curb its debilitating effects. Stewart Emery, a wonderful self-development facilitator, advises us to "take fear by the hand as a companion and move forward anyway." Even if we have to travel with this companion for a while, we will be able to move forward without letting it overwhelm us or limit our lives.

When we let go of the fear of being "wrong," or that another person will see our faults, we can begin to acknowledge our imperfections, to see that there are ways to learn and grow and gain the respect of those around us. As an example—a movie star drinks too much, admits

himself into a rehab clinic, and comes out clean. He pro-
fesses his error to the media and various talk-show hosts
who applaud his growth. The public sees him as a hero
for facing his problem, admitting his weakness, and taking responsibility for himself.

Other than the absence of media attention, are things
any different for us? No, in fact, they aren't. When we face
the obstacles that prevent us from living happily, when
we improve our lives, we are heroes, too. Once we meet
and greet our fear, learn about it, grow from the newly
acquired knowledge of ourselves, and let go of needing
to be seen in a "favorable" light, we too deserve applause
for being heroes. Every time we limit our lives with the
fear of being wrong, we have become its victim. When I
now ask myself, "Would I rather live a happy life as a
growing and heroic human being or would I rather be
directed by my fear?" My answer is "Embracing change
and valuing growth is where my hero lives." Try the next
exercise for taking fear by the hand as a companion and
meeting life head-on.

Creating Change: Take Fear by the Hand

The next time you feel afraid, imagine that the fear is a
shadow person standing beside you. See yourself taking
hold of this shadow's hand and walking together into the
experience. (Starting with smaller fears will give you time
to strengthen this imagery.) Now imagine yourself in the

feared situation saying to your shadow, "Come along with me. Yes, we are afraid, but we aren't going to let that stop us this time." It is better to meet and greet your fear than to let it prevent you from living your life.

Fair? Who Said Life Was Fair?

It's too bad that we weren't given an instruction book for living life. One of the most valuable pieces of information would have been "life is not fair." Had we known that from the beginning, we might have been able to let go of expecting things to be just or reasonable.

Even as children our expectations were that life would be fair. When it wasn't, our tear-soaked faces told of the injustices that had been forced upon us. As adults we have given up most of the public screaming and have had to internalize our reactions to sad, bad, and unfair happenings. We begin to tell our victim-victimizer stories to ourselves.

But bad things are going to happen to some of us and not to others. People are not always going to treat us the way we'd like them to. That's unfair. It's unfair when the people we love treat us badly because they don't understand what we have been through, what we know, or what we have done for them. It's unfair when we have to take the blame for another person's lies or been forced out of a job because of office politics. It's unfair to have been born with a genetic makeup that won't allow us to enjoy a healthy life.

We may not be able to do anything about the unfairness that comes into our lives, but we can do something about how we respond to it. We can look at our self-pity honestly and refuse to be its victim. How we handle life's difficulties says a lot about who we are. Dealing with the unfairness and adversities of life fully measures our heart, bravery, integrity, and humanity. This isn't a new idea.

> *'Tis easy enough to be pleasant,*
> *When life flows along like a song;*
> *But the man worthwhile is the one who will smile*
> *When everything goes dead wrong.*
> *For the test of the heart is trouble,*
> *And it always comes with the years,*
> *And the smile that is worth the praise of the earth,*
> *Is the smile that comes through tears.*
>
> —Ella Wheeler Wilcox, 1881

When it's time to deal with adversity, remember that the way we treat ourselves will help us reject our victim-victimizer stories and move on. If we stop eating well, use substances to deaden the pain, or go sleepless, we weaken our ability to handle the stress and choose our response to it. So when things are tough, try the following self-care program before moving forward. It is designed to give you some strength and distance from the difficult situation and soften your negative feelings.

Try this program for a week and notice your improvement grow.

Creating Change: Taking Care of Yourself

Do a strong, physical yoga practice, one that produces sweat and exercises the lungs. If you don't have a yoga practice, attend an aerobics class or swim for thirty minutes or more. After an intense workout, drink a glass of water and take a shower. While you are still wet, massage your whole body with sesame oil (use coconut oil if you are dealing with a lot of anger). Dry yourself off and drink another glass of water. Then lie down, cover yourself with a blanket, and do a deep relaxation for 15–20 minutes. Use a relaxation tape to make it easy on yourself. *Light Transitions Tapes* (see Reading and Resources) offers *Locate Your Space,* a good tape for dealing with fear and hurt feelings. Or try the tapes *Your Special Friend* or *For Your Health (Light Transitions Tapes),* which are effective with anger. Spend some time thinking about how you feel and how you want to respond. Note your progress and new ideas in your journal.

Our Focus Determines Our Results

Sometimes it's difficult to know exactly what our focus is, and until we are clear about it, we run the risk of slipping into the role of victim. On the superficial day-to-day level, we focus on the things that occupy our attention. But there is more to it, for beneath this level are the underlying ideas that drive our background thinking and make up our real focus. It is this real focus that determines our behavior. And our behavior determines the results we get in life.

Many people work hard for years to change their patterns of behavior without changing the thoughts, ideas, judgments, expectations, and/or prejudices that drive them. This won't work. The new replacement behavior patterns will only mirror the old ones because the real focus remains the same. When we want to make a change, we need to redirect our focus. Then our corresponding behavior will automatically change.

Instead of worrying about what other people think about us, we can focus on feeling good about ourselves. We cannot really control the way anyone else sees us. We can only make choices that let us behave in ways we can feel good about.

Creating Change: Focus Change

Take a long look at a recurrent problem you want changed in your life, and list the patterns of behavior that are directly related to it. Then discover the underlying ideas, objectives, or intentions that gave rise to the problem (the focus) by reflecting on how your thoughts have created your behavior.

When you have gathered as much information as you can, decide on the new results you want. Write them down. Think of the ideas, objectives, or intentions (the new focus) that will produce them. Then make the change in your focus! If you find yourself sliding back into your old focus, recommit to the change you have made. Do this as many times as it takes.

Self-Talk: Self-Soothing

How we talk to ourselves about an upsetting situation is important, for our self-talk affects our feelings, health, and self-esteem. The words we use in our minds to describe what happens to us define our ability to let go and move forward with our lives.

But there are times when we can't get the offender or the unfortunate event out of our minds, when we either can't or don't want to stop ourselves from going over and over the past event. We are obsessing. When we replay past words unremittingly or spend too much time rehearsing future conversations, our self-talk is out of control and we have become its victim.

At these times our self-talk is focused on blame, indictment, and resentment. Our minds are working against us. Our words are shaping our behavior and experience. But when we are aware of how our thinking is controlling us, we can change it. We can change our negative self-talk into self-soothing.

Replacing negative thinking (whether it is background thinking or conscious obsessing) with positive thoughts will help us see more objectively. Yoga offers a technique for making this change by means of a countermeasure—sometimes called "thinking on the opposite." The *Yoga Sutra* tells us that negative thinking is distorted thinking that will yield bitter fruits of endless sorrow and ignorance. It recommends practicing "contemplation on the opposite" to keep such sorrows away.

Remember—a glass can be seen as either half full or half empty. By focusing on fullness (or the positive), we can stop obsessing about the emptiness. We can stop being the victim of the past and go for the positive side of life.

To transform negative thinking, yoga masters often give their students *mantras* (a Sanskrit word or group of words) and instruct them to repeat it to themselves over and over. We can do this too with any word or group of words that elevates our minds, emotions, and spirits. Most of us already do this without realizing it, as when a phrase from a song begins to repeat endlessly in our minds. At that time, that phrase is a mantra. Replacing negative self-talk with positive words, or mantras, can help us transform negative thoughts about the past and turn fears about the future into a positive experience of the present.

Creating Change: Using a Mantra

Take charge. Change your thinking by creating a self-soothing mantra to replace conscious or unconscious negative self-talk. Make your mantra a positive statement. Select a word, a group of words, or short sentences that make you feel good or lighter. Any positive statement you like will work. (Avoid negating words, such as no, not, never, don't, can't, won't.) And once you have chosen your mantra, substitute it for all negative self-talk. Just keep repeating your new mantra as you go through your daily life. It works!

The Victim

Some people choose the victim role to handle small grievances or relationship problems. Some people's fear causes them to use the victim role as a way of life. Some feel like a "better" person in this role. They tell and retell their story to everyone— even to themselves.

> To be free, we have to let go of our grievance and our victim-victimizer story.

But when people don't let go and forgive, they condemn themselves to the role of victim—victims to past experiences and victims to the way they judge themselves. They give others power over them. They feel powerless, and become trapped in their own feelings. As a victim they have poor self-esteem and feel vulnerable and helpless to make changes. They have little joy. Not letting go, not forgiving holds them in this victim role.

On the other hand, if we have been injured and feel

pain, it is important to take time to grieve our losses—whether love, professional, self-esteem, friendship, or material. But remember, the false feelings of strength that come from reliving our victim-victimizer story will not counter its destructive impact of negativity and pain. And when we recognize the price we pay for holding on to the harmful thoughts and emotions of the past, we may be inspired to begin the liberating process of forgiveness.

chapter six

RELATIONSHIPS

MOST OF US THINK WE ARE in control of our immediate environment. This is an illusion. Most of us have difficulty controlling our own lives. But this illusion of control leads us to expect that the behavior of others will conform to our own ideas about what is right. It's as if we each watch our own "movie" of what is happening in the world, and when everyone is living from his or her own perspective, it is likely that the "movies" will not agree with one another. When they collide, there is usually pain.

One of yoga's basic principles is *ahimsa,* not causing pain, through our deeds, our words, and even our thoughts. By choosing not to inflict pain on anyone, including ourselves, the yoga masters tell us, we are choosing to live happier lives.

Relationships

Relationships range from mundane exchanges to intimate connections, from the authoritarian to the vacuous. And we handle each level differently. For instance, our closest friends may be able to challenge our behavior in ways that we would never allow a more distant connection to do. We may value something a stranger says to us but bristle if the same words are uttered by a parent. Our attachments, expectations, and the boundaries we establish differ for each type and level of relationship.

Relationships can be further complicated by fear. We can be afraid of confrontation, loss, rejection, being wrong, pain, or betrayal—to name a few. But one of the most widespread fears is that of being wrong and looking like a fool. People will go to great lengths to avoid letting anyone see their shortcomings. They know how they want to be perceived, and often they will sacrifice perfectly good relationships the first time their picture of themselves is threatened.

What is more, because we no longer grow up, live our whole lives, and die in the same town with the same people, we tend to treat our relationships as if they are disposable. We have access to more people and places and are less willing to stay in relationships if even the smallest problem arises, not realizing that when small problems are overcome, they become the ingredients for closer connections. Working through difficult experiences usually deepens and strengthens relationships.

To improve our associations with others, we have to

begin from the truth—from where we really are, not from where we want to think we are, and not from where we want others to think we are. Understanding what we fear is a good place to begin, for once we identify what we fear in a relationship, we can move forward with awareness. Remember, when fear interferes with our progress, understanding, or loving, it prevents us from experiencing the adventure and growth that defines life.

Relationships can also be affected by our body chemistry. Hormonal imbalances change our behavior and thinking—and therefore the way we relate to others. Even tiny chemical changes can cause big changes in us. In fact, someone once said, "We are all just a half-teaspoon away from being emotionally beleaguered." All of us have hormones that flux at different times and in different amounts. Women who have experienced drastic mood swings during a pregnancy have had a small taste of this truth. But some of us have to struggle with a hormonal imbalance for years or even entire lives. We are each unique, as is the behavior caused by our hormones.

Our brain chemistry can also be out of balance. Neurotransmitters (like serotonin) determine our thinking and "emotioning." If we have inherited a chemical imbalance in the brain, or if life has distorted the equilibrium we once had, controlling our behavior and thoughts may be challenging. This does not necessarily mean that we have psychological problems or that our life is a mess. It can simply mean that we have a malfunction, similar to a blood disorder or an organ dysfunction. And when this is the case, life is more difficult. Having a chemical imbalance just makes it harder to be comfortable and behave in relationships objectively or with total awareness. Sharon Cottor once described it as being like the person riding in coach while everyone else is riding first class.

Doing the Best We Can

People generally do the best they can with the provisions, emotional baggage, insights, talent, body chemistry, hardships, experiences, and emotional support available to them. We all do the best we can. We may feel we should have been able to do more, but that something was in our way. Something, often unknown, might very well have been stopping us—depression, fatigue, pain, low self-esteem, or the effects of a chemical imbalance. If we could do things differently to make our relationships better, most of us would.

Bill's wife was baffled because he spent so much of his time on the sofa watching sports while the house and yard were in need of repair. She thought Bill was just being lazy and could do more. She was right. Physically, he could have done more, but something was stopping him.

Bill told his therapist that he really did want to take care of the house and yard, but he just couldn't get himself up off the couch. His parents, he said, had repeatedly accused him of being lazy, useless, and a do-nothing, and now his wife was suggesting the same thing. He didn't care that much about sports, but he just couldn't make himself get off the couch.

When Bill and the therapist discussed Bill's past as well as his present feelings, Bill realized it wasn't that he had bad parents. He could see that they were strained and living out the expectations of their own parents (who had talked to them in this same way). He saw how people can become trapped in labels assigned to them by loved ones and end up living up to them.

We can want something to be different, but not be able to make the change. We may assign labels to our behavior, like "lazy," "incapable," or "high-strung," when our actions don't measure up to our ideas of how we "should be." But, like Bill, we may not have the ability to see the obstacles clearly. Immersed in depression and low self-esteem, Bill was doing the best he could. He finally realized that his parents would have treated anyone in his position the same way they had treated him, that it wasn't really personal. And when he was able to see that his parents had done their best and were simply reacting to their own lives, Bill was able to free himself from their influence and choose to act the way he wanted. He realized that it was their reaction to him, borne out of who they were at the time, that was the real cause of their treating him the way they did.

Creating Change: Change Your Experience

To change your experience, you must be willing to examine your own feelings and trace them back to their source. Use your journal to write about specific instances in your life that came to mind as you were reading this section. Take each instance individually. Spend time reflecting on what happened to you; examine your thoughts and feelings both at the time and since; and learn how your ideas, feelings, and behavior have changed as a result of your experience. Apply the ideas presented in this chapter to your situation and make a list of the things you can learn and the things you want to change.

> Everything is contextual. What is good in one society may be bad in another. Things that work in this generation may be unacceptable to the next.

Right or Wrong? Culture or Context?

Many people have been taught to think that everything in life is either right or wrong. We probably know people right now who are tied to the idea that they must always be right. They have to be right in order to feel good about themselves. When people are trained this way, they tend to think that wrong means inferior, substandard, or bad. If they had been persistently punished for being wrong when they were children, an even stronger tie to the idea of being right may have been forged and turned into a need.

But there are also those who have been downtrodden or taught to acquiesce. They rarely feel that they are right and apologize for mistakes they imagine they have made. They believe that if they had done "it" better or differently, things would have been OK. Others struggle to accept their own mistakes. Both those who acquiesce and those who deny fault are caught up in the "right and wrong" thinking model.

This right/wrong model of behavior limits our ability to know what is actually happening. Through its rigid structure, it can provide us with a sense of security, but this security is false, just as the idea that everything is black-or-white, right-or-wrong is false. Life situations are rarely so simple. More often they are made up of many shades of gray, each situation a matter of context and perspective.

The context in which an event happens is crucial to the way that event is seen. Right and wrong are determined by time, place, circumstances, and an ever-changing world of cultures. What is right in one particular time in history and in one particular culture may be wrong in another. Even when we are dealing with issues that we all agree are clearly wrong, if their context or the culture is changed, then wrong may become right. Thinking of a

family unit as a small culture, what is right in one household may not be in another:

> At Tina's house, gifts are a source of great
> fun. Family members make lists of things they
> would like as presents and give the lists to
> everyone who asks. And everyone does ask.
> They ask for lists before buying gifts, disguise
> the gifts with wrappings, and tease each oth-
> er about the presents that follow. They have
> a good time interacting in this way.
>
> When she married into Jim's family, Tina
> found that making "present lists" was frowned
> upon. In that culture, it was considered rude
> to express much interest in receiving pres-
> ents. Jim's family felt that being too involved
> in the process was in poor taste. Whenever
> Tina tried to talk about lists, tease, or even
> talk about presents to the members of Jim's
> family, she invariably walked away feeling
> diminished and put down.

Everyone involved in a situation sees it differently.
From our own perspective, other people's behavior may
seem strange. To them we may seem equally over-the-
top. But if we walk the right/wrong path and insist that
things must be done in only one specific way, we make
our own life's journey more difficult. Had Tina's and

Jim's families realized that differing points of view are neither good nor bad, they could have opened the door to better relationships.

Our perspectives shift with any change in culture. In fact, our perspectives naturally change with time, experience, need, and exposure. When we were younger, for example, we liked certain things that we no longer enjoy. Conversely, we disliked some things that we now take pleasure in. Dorrie is a good example of this:

> **To improve relation-ships, remember two things: change is the only constant in life and when the context changes, the meaning changes.**

At twenty, Dorrie hated smoked oysters. She vowed never to eat them as long as she lived and never to spend any serious time with anyone who did because she didn't like "oyster-breath." But in her thirties, after plenty of cocktail party exposure to oyster eating and validation from attractive men who ate them, Dorrie began to change her mind. Eventually she came to enjoy smoked oysters.

Dorrie's experience is a simple example of how tastes change, but this same premise holds true for issues far more complex than food. We grow into new, more experienced ways of life and change our beliefs, commitments, and opinions as we are exposed to more information and other people. Remembering that change is the only constant in life, and that ideas have different meanings in different contexts, can make our relationships easier.

The right/wrong path is fraught with obstacles that trip us up painfully, just like rocks on a road. Letting go of the right/wrong way of thinking frees us to enjoy a smoother, more comfortable trip through our life and relationships.

Creating Change: Ever-Changing Perspectives

Write down an example of something you disliked when you were younger, that you now like—or vice versa. Remember how clearly you felt your original opinion and how sure you were that you were right. When you have finished, write down how you feel now that your ideas have changed with maturity and experience. Reflect on the fact that both ideas belong to the same person—you.

Here is a simple example: Once I was praising a clothing store I loved when my perceptive daughter-in-law told me that she couldn't find much there that worked for her. She went on to say that while she liked the store, she thought our difference might be an age thing, and that the store was better suited to ages other than hers. At that moment, I remembered feeling the same way about that store when I was her age. But my current perspective was that it was the only store I ever needed to go into again. It was fun and freeing to experience two opposite opinions—both mine—at the same time. Remembering the ever-changing nature of opinions, ideas, and perspectives can help eliminate the right/wrong trap.

Acknowledging Our "Stuff"

To understand the way forgiveness affects difficult relationships, we must uncover the part we played in creating them and take an objective look at the details. No blame or fault need be assigned. The problems are usually found in the relationship itself and rarely in the people involved. Dr. Seanna Adamson, a noted equestrian and sports psychologist, explains this point well:

> We all come with "stuff" that is in our hardwiring, but while a person's "stuff" may be a problem for me, it may not be a problem for someone else. As an example, let's say I have a horse that is really powerful. Each time I ride him, he overpowers me. Because of the way I respond to him, he learns that he can be "dominant" in our relationship. But if a big strong man that he cannot overpower rides him, their relationship will be completely different because the man's responses to the horse will be different. Likewise, I may get a lot of work out a very sensitive horse while another, more powerful rider might not be able to get in

touch with the horse's needs well enough to
support a good relationship between them.

People show up for a relationship with all their hardwiring in place, and this is what interacts to create a relationship. How our hardwiring responds to another person's
hardwiring determines what happens next and makes an
impact on how well the relationship works. So it only
makes sense to ask ourselves some questions about the
part we played in a discordant situation.

It is important for us to take responsibility for our
responses. We don't necessarily have to acknowledge this
to anyone else, but it is important that we know for ourselves where, when, and how we could have contributed
to a problem or how we could have responded differently.

Even when it appears that the "offenders" are clearly
wrong, we still need to look at the part we played in the
conflict. (Please note: this section does not apply to anyone who has been the victim of a criminal offense.) For
instance, did we hide the fact that we were hurt? Did we
egg our opponent on in some way? Were we truthful
about how we felt or did we back away? Did we let them
off the hook or did we demand that they accept responsibility for their actions? Did we stay in the situation when
we should have left it or did we leave when we should
have stayed? What did we say or do that "they" could have
found hurtful? Did we do anything that we don't feel good
about? In order to forgive and move on, we need to be

honest and clear about the part we played in a discordant situation. On the other hand, there are those who feel too responsible, who take on responsibility for most, if not all the behavior around them when it should be shared. These people need to look at themselves carefully. No one can be responsible for another person's hardwiring.

As we take a closer look at ourselves and the role we play in conflicts, we will see ourselves more clearly, and thus begin to move out of the victim role and into the learning mode. This will make us stronger and more able to take better care of ourselves in future situations.

Creating Change: The Letter

Write letters to those who offend you, letters that you will not send. First make a list of their positive qualities, and then write down everything they have done for you and how you benefited from your relationship with them. Then tell them (in the letter) how you could have responded to the hurtful situation differently. Remember not to take on the burden of how "they would be a better person if only . . ." Focus on what you have learned from yourself and your words, thoughts, and actions. End your letters by saying you are on a healing journey of forgiveness and that this letter is a part of that process.

They Probably Did Their Best

If we have been hurt, we tend to think that others should have behaved differently. But we can't really know their capacity. Many people blame their parents for not doing as good a job raising them as they believe they could have. But as much as we may want our parents to have been different, they probably couldn't have been. After all, they are also a product of their upbringing. We deserved better, yes, but they probably did too. How long can we blame and punish someone for being what they were trapped into being?

As a child, Paul felt powerless to change his situation. He was the son of a poor, single mother who worked 10 hours a day outside the home. Paul believed that he should have had a family like the ones he saw on television. But without any family support system, his mother worked, cleaned, shopped, chauffeured, and loved him. To this day, however, Paul remains angry that she did not give him "what every child should have"—a model family. Without a father in the household or nearby relations to help keep Paul's perspective in focus, he never learned to honor, appreciate, or respect his mother for what she did do. He only begrudges what he thinks he missed. Paul has carried these negative feelings for decades and has left his relationship with his mother behind.

If we look back through the generations, we see that the rules, ideas, and practices for each were different according to the thinking of the time. For example, we cannot apply present-day child-rearing ideas to past generations. That would take the situation out of its context. Remember that to see clearly, everything must be judged in its own context. If we are having trouble forgiving our parents, we may be able to gain some perspective by taking a closer look at the life they had. (In most cases it was more difficult than ours.) When we understand the circumstances that made them the way they were, we take our first steps on the road to forgiveness and freedom. It can be helpful to remember some important points we have covered previously:

- Problems between two people stem from the relationship itself, not from the people involved in it.
- When we label, blame, and accuse people for what they have done, or should have done to us, we are acting from the illusion that there is only one perspective and we are right while they are wrong.
- We cannot learn and grow by insisting that we are right.
- Armed with our victim-victimizer story, we may persuade others to believe in our cause and create a following that believes our grievance is the other person's fault and we are innocent, but reliving this negativity will only harm us.

Sure, our mothers (fathers, aunts, lovers, wives, husbands, sisters, brothers, friends, bosses, co-workers) might not have given us what we think they should have. They may have treated us unfairly, used us, hurt us, and made our life seem horrible. We may still be upset because we think that we deserved more. But whether we have been treated poorly or not, right now we are the only ones who can repair the damage. It is our responsibility to make whatever changes are needed to nurture happy, healthy lives and relationships.

If we don't do this, the only suffering will be ours—in both the immediate experience and from the adrenaline and other angry, fight-or-flight chemicals the body generates every time the same experience is repeated. Even if we think "they" have not suffered enough for what they have done to us, we certainly have. And this means it is time to change our thinking. We can free ourselves by realizing that "they" couldn't have done any better than they did.

> Right now we are the only one who can repair our lives. It is our responsibility to make the changes that will nurture happy, healthy lives and relationships.

Creating Change: Let's Get Relative

Our pain and suffering are real. They should not be minimized by others or ourselves. There are times when we may be overwhelmed with pain or so absorbed in

our own sorrow that we no longer experience the rich-
ness of life. When it seems as if there is no more to life
than the pain we are in, we can try to see our problems
in relation to others in the world. This is a diverting technique that can move us out of suffering and into a
healthier frame of mind—at least for a few moments.

Think of the millions of people who struggle every day
with famine, death, and disease—people who would be happy to have our lives, even with the pain we feel right now.
Look at the suffering and pain in the world; starvation, war,
enslavement, death, destruction, and despair are everywhere.
Remember the pictures of the small African children lying
emaciated, covered with flies, open sores, and filth, with only
hours or days to live? Imagine the pain of the mothers, rela-
tives, and friends who are helpless to save them.

In the long run, it is vital that we not minimize our loss,
pain, or struggle, but we may find some temporary relief
when we remember the horror that other people face daily. It may help us stop just long enough to step outside of
ourselves, put our pain in perspective, and see the good
parts of our lives.

No Apology Needed

When we have been harmed, we want to know why
those who offended us did what they did. We wait,
demand, hope, or lobby for their apology or at least some
sign of repentance. (And because it relieves some of the
pain and anger, an apology can make forgiving easier.)

Sometimes we may even say to ourselves, "There is no way I am going to forgive unless they say they are sorry and admit their fault." But even though it would be nice to receive an apology, it is not a prerequisite for the forgiveness process.

Waiting for other people to admit they have done something that hurt us leaves us in the role of victim. And as we wait for an apology, we remain imprisoned in the past and at the mercy of the "offender." When we refuse to move forward until our demands are met, we leave our happiness and health in the hands of the offender. We cling to the past—sometimes for years—creating endless pain for ourselves and others. This is not necessary. The fact is that we really don't need an apology. We don't need to understand why "they" acted as they did in order to forgive them. And we don't need to continue our relationship with them. We only need to let go of the past and move on.

Creating Change: Communication Skills

There are many communication skills that can be very helpful in improving relationships, but they can be better-learned through classes and books dedicated to their subject. Classes, offered in most community colleges and local city catalogs, are a good resource. Look for courses in communication, and the identification of "emotioning" words. The book or DVD *Nonviolent Communication,* by Marshall Rosenberg, is another good resource for learning and understanding how to communicate.

chapter seven

DETACHING, ACCEPTING, DECIDING

TWO OF YOGA'S MOST IMPORTANT practices are concentration and non-attachment. Through concentration we gain what yogis call a one-pointed mind (what we call focus). Through non-attachment we detach, or disconnect the mind from its personal desires (what we call letting go). Both are essential for the process of forgiveness.

Through focus we gain the discipline to live by our standards, the ability to make the choices that release us from pain, and the openness to see both disturbing situations and our responses to them clearly. Focus keeps us concentrated objectively in the present instead of being constantly influenced by old ideas and past reactions. Maintaining a concentrated focus gives us the ability to control our thoughts, words, and feelings.

In yoga, non-attachment does not mean distancing ourselves from others or becoming cold or indifferent. It means virtually the same thing as letting go. Through detachment we gain the ability to release ourselves from harmful situations, negative feelings and ideas, and excessive ego needs. By letting go we learn to take things less personally and remember that unconscious behavior and mistakes happen all the time. We don't need to attach ourselves to them.

All human beings act unconsciously and make mistakes. It's human nature. All human beings are oblivious at times just as all human beings have periods of wisdom. Problems arise when we judge ourselves by our wisest, most mindful moments, but judge our enemies by their mistakes and unconscious moments. It is possible to change this. Over time and through practice, we can develop our abilities to detach and focus, and in the process we will learn to accept what is and make effective decisions.

A Set of Standards: The Yamas and Niyamas

The *yamas* and the *niyamas* are yoga's standards for living happily. They serve as reference points during times of confusion, misdirection, and ignorance. When in doubt about a course of action, we can refer to these standards and be reminded of honest, ethical behavior and be inspired to act in better ways than we might otherwise choose.

In Patanjali's *Yoga Sutra*, the first of the eight "limbs" of yoga, the *yamas*, consists of five ethical disciplines: non-violence *(ahimsa)*, truth *(satya)*, non-stealing *(asteya)*, regulation of the senses *(brahmacharya)*, and non-coveting *(aparigraha)*. When we adhere to these ethical standards, we experience new strength and better self-esteem. We become more comfortable with ourselves and the world. Following the yamas, the yogis tell us, will eliminate the problems created by man's natural tendency toward violence, deception, theft, greed, and egotism.

The second limb of yoga, the *niyamas,* consists of five attitudes of mind that lead to a healthy, happy life: cleanliness *(saucha)*, contentment *(santosha)*, discipline *(tapas)*, self-study *(svadhyaya)*, and dedication to a force greater than our individual self—whether it be nature, light, or God *(ishvarapranidhana)*. The niyamas teach us to care for ourselves through cleanliness of mind and body, contentment with reality, discipline in our practice, and awareness of the wholeness of being. Self-study *(svadhyaya)* is the way to see ourselves more clearly by discovering how we perceive and interact with the world and by studying the wisdom handed down in important philosophical books. Following the niyamas will improve our health on all levels—physical, mental, emotional, and spiritual.

When our lives are filled with thoughts and actions that support our health, relationships, and self-esteem, we give ourselves the best possible chance for living happily. Following the yamas and niyamas can bring order, understanding, peace, honesty, discipline, and respect for life and property to every individual as well as to society as a whole. The yamas and niyamas are excellent tools for the practice of forgiveness.

Creating Change: Examining the Yamas
and Niyamas

By spending time reflecting and writing on each of the five yamas, you can learn to see yourself more clearly and choose to make positive changes that will make you feel good about yourself. Begin with the yama non-violence—not just of our actions, but also in our words and thoughts. Reflect on the violence happening right now in your life and in the world. Try writing down all the violent thoughts, words, and actions you have in one 24-hour period.

As you look at this list, as well as at your behavior in relation to each of the yamas and niyamas, remember that we are all human, and to some extent this is how human beings are. This exercise is designed for you to see yourself more clearly, so no recriminations, judgments, or admonishments, please. Just learn from what you see.

Accepting What Is

If we want to be happy, it is essential that we accept life as it is. The struggle to try to make things different from the way they are, wanting what we don't or can't have, and the battle to control the uncontrollable all create suffering. It is true that accepting "what is" may not cancel out our pain, but it will make it easier to live with. Not accepting reality becomes an ongoing battle that can only end in defeat. (Acceptance, however, does not mean that we should lie down and do nothing if we are being abused. We need to take care of ourselves, and we

must *always* remove ourselves from physical or psychological battery.)

Who Is Responsible?

If we have been in a hurtful
situation, we can find ourselves
stuck somewhere between
regret, guilt, loss, and anger and
feel strongly that it is someone
else's responsibility to make
things better. To let go of being
victim to these circumstances,

> Wanting what we
> cannot have,
> struggling to control
> the uncontrollable,
> and trying to change
> the unchangeable
> creates suffering.

we have to give up wanting others to admit they were
wrong. Remember—we can move on without that. We
don't need their apology to practice forgiveness.
Forgiveness is our own responsibility.

When an upsetting event has taken place, it has happened, and now it's over. That is the end of it unless we
rationalize the situation and continue to carry feelings and
thoughts that blame others. The fact that we have been
treated badly in the past does not make it someone else's
job to repair the damage. It is our responsibility to pick up
the ball and move forward in our own way. It's our life
that is being affected.

But now, at this moment, we are the ones who are
keeping alive the memory of what was wrong. If at this
moment we are the ones who are hurting, hating, lament-
ing, complaining, or blaming, we are not really living this

moment; we are living in the past. And when we do this, our life is not our own. It has been lost to rehashing what has already taken place.

Now is now. When we don't live in this moment, it is gone. If we don't forgive, we are using up these brief times of potential experience to stay attached to past suffering or anger. Why? Is it going to make us feel better? Or will it help make the villains in our story pay? No. The only one who pays is the one who is entertaining the thoughts that initiate negative responses in the body's chemistry. Each time we rehash an upsetting experience, the only suffering will be from the adrenaline and other fight-or-flight chemicals that our body generates. We are the only ones who can end this. Every time we blame, complain, and strain over events that are long past, we can stop and focus our attention on this moment. By doing so, we step away from the past and come into the present.

Creating Change: Redirection Therapy

When you find your thoughts or emotions focused on a past problem, stop immediately and bring your attention to your breath. Breathe in, now. Breathe out, now. Stay focused on this moment. Feel the environment, feel your body, look at your surroundings. Do whatever you need to bring your attention back into this minute. Break the habit of reliving the painful past. Remember to be where you really are—here and now.

What Does It All Mean?

Realizing that we are not irreparably damaged, that we can move on, is a part of the forgiveness process. And realizing that we can give up the victim mentality and reframe our perspective gives strength to our efforts. One way to do this is to find some meaning in the upsetting experience and grow from it.

Finding meaning in suffering brings people to a new understanding about what has happened to them. They are more able to deal with their pain because they have learned something valuable from the experience, so it wasn't all for nothing. Psychotherapist Viktor Frankl, who developed a psychotherapeutic approach to suffering, describes the search for meaning this way in *Man's Search for Meaning*:

> The noblest appreciation of meaning is reserved for those who, by the very attitude that they choose to bring to this predicament, rise above it and grow beyond themselves. What matters is the stand they take—a stand that allows for the transmutation of their predicament into achievement, triumph, and heroism.

"What can I learn from this painful experience?" we might ask ourselves. "How has it changed me? Has it made me more sensitive, stronger, braver, or more mature? What did I learn about people or situations that I can use to improve my life?" Everyone finds meaning in his or her own way, and no matter how great the suffering, there is usually a lesson to be learned or meaning to be found that will salve the wounds. If this is too difficult to see at first—stay open. Later in the process of forgiving, another perspective may arise that provides some useful insight. It isn't necessary to do this, of course, but finding meaning can make the pain easier to bear.

Creating Change: Keep Journaling

Using your journal, make a list of the changes that have come as a result of your painful experience. Describe how you have grown, what you have gained, and how you can transform negative experiences in the future. Feel good about yourself for making the choice to learn and grow.

Find the Upside

Every situation has a positive and negative side, and we can choose to find the positive or the negative in almost every situation. As an example, winning the lottery seems like a wholly positive experience, but it also has a down side. We expect winners of millions of dollars to be overjoyed, but new research shows that these elevated highs diminish our ability to re-experience them, that after the "big win" it takes about ten percent more to stimulate the same happiness they originally felt. There can be other negative effects, too. We cannot be sure if new friends are with us because we are rich or because they like us. And it can be harder to get the truth from people because money influences their judgment. Just as a positive experience can have its downside, so can a painful experience have an upside. If nothing else, it can teach us valuable lessons when we choose to look for something positive.

> Life feels better when we can look for lessons from difficult situations and see the positive (no matter how small it may be).

Is a disturbing situation half positive or half negative? It's all a matter of what we choose to see. To keep the positive side of things in view, look for what can be learned, see the good intentions in others, recognize our own positive intentions, give up feeling victimized, and try to see the beauty and love that is everywhere.

Instead of focusing on what we don't have, we can look at what we do have. Try this with small things first. For example, when it's time to take out the garbage, we can silently thank the garbage men for coming to take it away from the house. We can thank the sanitation department for organizing trash disposal so that we don't have to put it in the car, drive it to the dump ourselves, pay a dump fee, unload it, and return home. Try it. It works!

Creating Change: Being Thankful for the Positive

Each evening write a gratitude list of ten things you are thankful for on this day. Make each day's list different from the previous days. With just a little reflection, you will find many small, positive things (a flower, a kind word, a look) unique to that day. Work with the techniques in Chapter 4 to help stay on the positive side of life.

Cleansing the Mind

How many times has the memory of an unpleasant encounter slid back into our minds? Rather than resolve these old conflicts, we try to forget them, but our emotions bind them to us. And when we have accumulated a lot of them, it can feel like a swarm of mosquitoes buzzing in our minds. They may only bite once in a while, but they are distracting. Even when we are not focused on them directly, they are like a background sound we can blank out until we don't know we're hearing it. But even though we may not be aware of it, we are still using our energy to blank them out. And if the swarm is large enough, it's hard to concentrate or relax. We may not know why this is happening. But it is.

Life is easier when our minds are free of distracting memories. We can concentrate better, completely relax, and feel more energetic. We have nothing to lose and everything to gain by cleaning up our mind's background pollution.

Creating Change: Cleansing the Mind

The way to keep ourselves free of old disturbing thoughts and to free up the energy we waste trying to ignore them is to meticulously resolve them one by one. This is a constructive and satisfying way to clean up the mind. It takes only a few minutes each day.

Think of a past wound that keeps coming into your mind, an old one that only surfaces occasionally, and deal with it with a visualization. Use the imagery that works best for you. For example, imagine sifting through a bowl of beans, taking out the bad ones and disposing of them. In the same way, take each hurtful thought, look at it, review it, and then see yourself picking it up and moving it out of your mind. Dispose of it. You can make up your own visualization. Think of one that appeals to you and practice using it to cleanse your mind for a few minutes every day.

Deciding to Forgive

Consciously deciding to let go of our negativity and forgive is crucial to the forgiveness process. Sometimes the decision comes from a change of heart, or a change in perspective. Sometimes it comes from accepting responsibility, or committing to happiness. And sometimes it comes from understanding that letting go of negativity is more important and healthful than holding onto it. No matter how we get to the decision point, the important thing is that we arrive. Even if the decision is halfhearted at first, we need to commit to walking away from our negative feelings and moving on with our lives. That decision will strengthen and support our willingness to forgive.

It requires strength to separate ourselves from our negativity. The decision to do this is challenging even when we are not steeped in resentment, anger, or grief. When we decide to forgive, we have to give up our victim story and lose the validation its retelling has brought us. We also have to let go of the ideas of being right, making the offender wrong, getting our way, retribution, and being saved by someone else. No matter how hard it is, by doing this we will free ourselves from the past and be able to live happier lives. Remember—being happy is the best revenge. The following technique uses symbolism to help strengthen your resolve to forgive.

Creating Change: **An Act of Symbolism**

Look at your own situation as you approach the point of making your decision to forgive. First ask yourself honestly if what you have been doing up to this point has worked. Are you happy? Repressing pain and anger is not going to work, so it's time to turn things around. Use the information in this book to help you find a way to make a change in your perspective or even a change of heart. Then try performing a symbolic act of forgiveness to carry you through.

For example, you could write all of your reasons for not forgiving on a paper and then burn it. While the paper is burning, imagine that your anger and hurt are bursting into nothingness in the flames.

Another symbolic act might be to plant a forgiveness tree or bush to exemplify your commitment. Plant it in a place where you will see it regularly. As it grows, it will be a daily reminder of your strength, growth, and pledge. Inviting someone else to witness your symbolic act of forgiveness can make it even more meaningful.

chapter eight

MORE WAYS TO CREATE CHANGE

THIS CHAPTER IS DEVOTED to a few Western adaptations of traditional yoga techniques. They will improve your ability to forgive the past and remain fully aware and alive in the present moment. Select the ones that feel right for you and use them as suggested. Don't worry about the others. By choosing several, you can build a daily practice of self-development and transformation. This is the path to letting go and being happy. And don't forget the yamas and niyamas described in Chapter 7.

Try Silence

Practicing silence for a few hours (or even a whole day) every week can be immensely rewarding. Some students have said, "Oh, I can't be quiet that long," but after trying it, they not only found that they could, they also enjoyed it. They were surprised at how easy and transformative the practice was. It literally changed their lives.

When students observe silence regularly, they find they are able to see the workings of their mind. They find they can observe the mental instructions they constantly give themselves, their ongoing judgments and evaluations, and the mind's usual overactivity. Silence gives them an experience of groundedness, contentment, peace, and clarity. It's so rewarding that it is well worth a try.

Technique: First, you have to decide that you want to observe silence regularly. Assign a time slot and a block of time you can devote to a regular practice, and use the same day and time every week. Here are two examples: all day every Wednesday, or every Thursday morning until 11 a.m. It's easier to remember to maintain silence if you begin the first thing in the morning. And since it takes about four sessions to be comfortable with it, make a contract with yourself to continue the practice weekly for two months.

I practiced observing silence for ten years, most of that time on Tuesdays. When I went to bed Monday evening, I stopped talking until I woke up Wednesday morning. I thought of that period as my time of renewal and nourishment. Whenever possible, I spent the day doing things around the house and giving extra time to reading, my yoga practice, or writing. I tried to be completely silent and not communicate with my eyes or actions, either. But when I couldn't devote the day to myself, I would interact with the world as necessary—just not with my mouth. If I needed to go out to lunch, attend a meeting, work, or run errands, I would.

Surprisingly, it was easy to communicate with the world without words. Hand gestures, facial expressions, and head nodding covered almost all of my communication needs. I made a point of carrying paper and pen with me, but I didn't need them most of the time. I wrote notes when I wanted to give specific information. People who knew that I was observing silence enjoyed the idea of it. The people who didn't know thought I had lost my voice.

For emergencies you can write messages. Many of today's "silent yogis" use small chalkboards they always carry. People don't mind, and most of them won't notice. It's surprising. So as a way to get to know yourself better and increase your energy, contentment, and sense of delight, try observing silence on a regular basis.

Yoga Vision: Soft Eyes

Learning to see everything within your field of vision all at once is called "seeing with soft eyes." This yoga vision widens our experience. It brings our attention to a larger area around us and creates more awareness of ourselves as a small part of a whole. Try it. It's easy.

Technique: Instead of looking directly at a specific thing, try to see the whole field of vision at the same time—the sides, top, bottom, and background. To do this, sit or stand with an erect spine, hold your eyes still, and widen your gaze by using your peripheral vision.

I often augment this technique by trying to imagine that my vision originates from a point at the back of my head or spine as I see and interact with the world. In my workshops, I call this "seeing with the back body." Driving, operating machinery, etc., are not good times to practice this soft focus, but standing in line, sitting in a waiting room, having lunch alone, or sitting in a meditative position are excellent times to do it. This simple practice can change your experience of life and bring a sense of peace.

Pranayama: Breath Control Practices

Many philosophies and religions equate the breath with spirituality, perhaps because breathing is the source of life. When breathing stops, life stops. In fact, the yoga masters tell us that the breath is the only link between our spirit, mind, emotions, and physical body. Because of this link, the breath mirrors our feelings and thoughts. When we become excited (whether for a positive or a negative reason), our breath becomes faster and shallower. The more excited we are, the faster our breathing. And if we intentionally breathe rapidly, our bodies and minds will be stimulated. On the other hand, when we can control our breathing, slowing it down and returning it to normal at will, we can change our emotions as well as our thoughts. When our breathing is even and smooth, we are in a relaxed, comfortable state. Thus, if we learn to control our breath, we can change ourselves effectively on every level.

The ancient yogis used a number of breathing exercises, or pranayama, to alter their energy and consciousness. Try the following exercises to help manage negative thoughts and feelings.

Ujjayi Breath (Glottal Sound to Calm and Soothe)

Technique: With the mouth slightly open, inhale and exhale slowly, making a *ah* or *ha* sound. The vocal cords do not make this sound. It is a breath sound (softer but similar to the sound Darth Vader made in *Star Wars*). It comes from the throat where it is intentionally restricted by slightly closing the glottis (contracting the throat muscle). With this partial closing, the movement of air is slowed and an even, soothing sound is made.

When the throat is slightly closed, it feels as if you are about to yawn. Continue inhaling and exhaling with the mouth still slightly open until you have mastered the sounds. Continue making the *ah* and *ha* sounds and slowly close the mouth. When the mouth is completely closed, the inhalations make a slightly different sound, a soft *sa* sound, and the exhalations make a soft *ha* sound. Take your time. Work with this until you can control the breath consistently and maintain even, steady breath sounds. Then practice for 3–10 minutes (or as long as needed) every day. This breathing with the *ujjayi* sound calms the body, mind, and emotions by controlling the flow of breath in and out of the lungs.

Nadi Shodhanam (Alternate Nostril Breathing)

Technique: Inhale through both nostrils. Close the right nostril with the thumb of the right hand and exhale slowly and completely through the left nostril. Inhale through the left nostril. Then close the left nostril with the ring finger and release the thumb from the right nostril. Exhale through the right nostril. Inhale through the right nostril. Then close the right nostril with the thumb and release the ring finger from covering the left nostril. This is one round of alternate nostril breathing, *nadi shodhanam.* To center the mind and emotions, practice five to ten rounds. (For more information, see Reading and Resources: *Light Transitions Tapes.*)

Back Body Breathing

One of the easiest ways to take control of your life is to take control of your breath, for when you control the breathing, you control the emotions and the mind. Back Body Breathing is one of the most effective ways to practice breath control. It increases your awareness of yourself and everything going on around you, and you can practice it no matter where you are or what you are doing. Try it in a quiet sitting position until you have mastered it (about twenty to thirty days). Then you will be ready to move the practice into your daily life as you stand, sit, or talk with friends.

Technique: Sit or stand with a straight back. If you are seated, rest your hands on your knees, palms up. If you are standing, let your arms and hands hang restfully at your sides. Close your eyes and bring your attention into your body and your breath. Exhale completely. As you inhale, let the top of your head move a few inches toward the floor (like looking down) and round your upper back slightly. Continue the slight rounding of your back from the upper through the middle and all the way down to your tailbone as your inhalation progresses. When you exhale, straighten your back, starting from the bottom, until you are lengthening your neck (the top of your head moves upward, reaching toward the ceiling).

With every inhalation, let the spine round slightly and evenly from the neck down to the tailbone. Make it feel as if you are opening your back to receive the inhalation. With every exhalation, straighten and extend the spine upward from the tailbone to the top of the head. Feel as if you are lifting the chest and spine straight upward to give out the exhalation. Think of the giving and receiving that takes place with each breath as you practice for 5–15 minutes with your eyes closed. Notice how you feel when you have finished each session. In times of stress, do this practice four or more times a day.

When the practice has become second nature (twenty-five to thirty consecutive days), make the movements of the spine smaller and smaller until they are so small that other people would not notice them. At that point, only think of widening the back and opening each section of the spine with the inhalation. Feel the skin on each side of the spine as it widens out to the sides. Then think of grounding the base of the spine into the floor as you stretch each vertebrae upward on the exhalation. This easy practice can change your life!

Healing Visualizations

Healing images in the mind can transform negative thoughts and emotions. When you feel angry, sad, or heartbroken, for example, you can use one of the many visualization tapes on the market today that guide you through a process of relaxation and healing. Or you can try practicing the following relaxation/visualization exercise by yourself.

Technique: Lie down on a bed or the floor (with a mat) and make yourself comfortable. Cover yourself lightly to make sure you remain warm (remember that your temperature goes down with deep relaxation), and take a few minutes to relax each part of the body before you begin the visualization. Start at the feet and work your way toward the head, and as you bring your mind to each part of the body, ask it to relax. You may want to slowly and silently repeat, "I am relaxed," to help let go of all sensation in the body.

After you are completely relaxed, imagine yourself in a nurturing, healing, pleasant place. Some people like to imagine that they are lying in a bath of something like warm cream or honey. The warmth relaxes them and soothes away their aches and sorrows, and they imagine themselves soaking up the nourishing and restorative power of the cream or honey. If this does not feel right to you, select any image for your visualization that is quietly appealing and nurturing.

After you have chosen your image, relax. Then ease into it and let your body, mind, emotions, and spirit be fed there for 10–20 minutes. When you feel restored, imagine each part of the body waking up revitalized. Inhale, and slowly stretch your body. Bend your left knee, turn over on your right side, and use your arms to push yourself up to a seated position. (For more information, see Reading and Resources: *Light Transitions Tapes* and Norman Shealy's *90 Days to Self-Health*.)

Gaining Strength: Clearing the Mind

According to the yoga masters, when we are resting in our own true nature, we are in a state of happiness or contentment *(santosha)*. We achieve this state through clarity of mind. It is our thoughts, the yogis tell us, that interfere with our ability to reach this state. Too many distressing ideas weaken our mental focus, and this results in indecisiveness as well as the inability to control ourselves or support our own best interests. Here is a way to begin the clarification process.

Preparation: Designate a place where you can sit in silence without being disturbed. Choose a chair or cushion in a quiet corner out of the flow of foot traffic. Place a pen and paper close by to make a note of any realization you have about your forgiveness process that takes place during your practice. You may want to bring a candle to light (for the length of each sitting) to represent the light and focus that you are bringing into your life. Plan to sit there once or twice a day for 10–30 minutes each time. (The longer you sit, the more effective the practice can be.) Once you have found and prepared your sitting place and committed to a regular block of time for sitting, you are ready to begin the daily practice of clearing the mind.

Technique: Begin by settling yourself into a comfortable sitting position with your spine straight (vertical). Once you are settled, be prepared to sit without moving. Clear your mind of all thoughts and simply watch the movement of the life force (the breath, or *prana*) as it enters and leaves your body. Remember that each inhalation brings new life to every cell, and each exhalation eliminates the waste products of metabolism. This leaves the body cleaner and more relaxed than it was before you began the exercise. Try seeing and feeling this process as it happens in your body.

Each time concentration on your breath is interrupted by a thought, stop and assign that thought to a category you make up. For instance, if you think, "The dog needs a bath," you may want to put that thought into a category named "Dog" or "Pets." Imagine placing the category four or five feet above your head. After the category is in place, imagine taking the thought out of your mind and putting it up into the category—then return to witnessing your breath. Repeat this process with every thought that enters your mind: create a name for the category, place it above your head, and put the thought there. Be gentle with yourself. Don't judge how many thoughts are interrupting your concentration on the breath. Just return your attention to the breath after you have disposed of each thought.

Concentration and Meditation

The next step in clearing the mind is really one practice—concentration automatically becomes meditation after a strong point of focus has been developed and sustained for an extended period of time. We know that our houseplants need water in order to grow and flourish. When we water and fertilize them regularly, they stay healthy and strong. In the same way, a regular concentration/meditation practice is like watering and fertilizing our body/mind.

One of the great benefits of concentration is the nurturing effect it has on us. When the mind becomes still, the body will balance and heal itself naturally. By regularly practicing concentration, we give ourselves what we need in order to learn, grow, and flourish. Focusing on the breath is especially beneficial, for each inhalation brings new life to every cell in the body, while every exhalation cleanses the entire system. The following concentration/meditation practice is a good technique for both new and more experienced meditators.

Technique: Sit without moving and witness your breathing. Clear your mind of all thoughts, judgments, and evaluations. Simply watch your body as it inhales and exhales. After one complete breath, silently say to yourself, "one." But to count a breath as "one," you will need to complete one whole inhalation and exhalation without having a single thought. If a thought arises, simply return to zero and begin again. If it takes a long time before you are able to count to one, it doesn't matter. The idea is to teach the mind to be still and that takes time. So be patient. Remember—we have to brush our teeth, cut the grass, clean the kitchen, and wash the floors over and over again. It is the same with the mind. We have to bring the mind back to what we choose for our focus over and over again until we have control of it. If possible, do this for 15–20 minutes once or twice each day.

JOURNEY'S END

LIFE IS NOW—THIS MINUTE, THIS SECOND. There is no time to waste. Living a life of reaction rather than response, a life filled with expectation, attachment, and inattention, is like going to the finest restaurant in the world and letting your waiter sit down, order, and eat your dinner. You miss the experience that belonged to you.

Imagine being in a place where everything is wonderful but you don't experience it because you are using your time to reenact past torment. Your life should be yours. You don't have to be the victim of the past. You have the ability to change it.

What you do with your life, how you decide to live it, is up to you. You do have control. Take it! You may have to wrestle some old habits or ideas down to the ground to get your control back, but with a firm decision and a clear commitment, you can do it. You can decide to be the person you want to be by choosing the way you interpret every moment of your daily experience. So make the commitment now to choose the focus that will create the experience you want. Relentlessly choose happiness.

If a life of satisfaction and happiness is what you want, you need to be committed to staying in the present moment rather than being trapped in past experiences, unable to get free from memories of painful situations. You need to free yourself by focusing on the positive happenings in your life. The moment-to-moment happiness leads to the abiding sense of joy and peace the ancient yoga masters discovered. You can attain it, too. Why not begin right now?

Remember, you are the beneficiary of letting go. Forgiveness is a gift you give yourself every time you practice it. Detaching from past negative and painful experiences will make you feel freer, more positive, healthier, and give you more energy for living. You can do it. It just takes processing and practice. In time, you will be so good at forgiving, you will be able to forgive it all as it happens and live in the experience of NOW—the home of abiding happiness.

A Final Tale

A wonderful seminar trainer and facilitator, Stewart Emery, used to say, "Only a fool speaks before the end." Here is a short story that illustrates his point:

Two friends were walking in the desert. At some point in their journey, they had an argument and one friend slapped the other on the face. The one who was slapped was hurt, but without saying a word, he wrote in the sand:

Today my best friend slapped me on the face.

The friends kept on walking until they found an oasis where they decided to bathe. The one who got slapped got stuck in the mire and started to drown, but his friend came to his rescue and saved him. After recovering from the near drowning, he wrote on a stone:

Today my best friend saved my life.

The friend who had slapped and saved his best friend said to him, "After I hurt you, you wrote in the sand. Now, you write on a stone. Why?" His friend replied, "When someone hurts us we should write it down in the sand where the winds of forgiveness can erase it away. But when someone does something good for us, we must engrave it in stone where no wind can ever erase it."

Life is better when we write our hurts in the sand and carve each positive moment in stone.

IMPORTANT POINTS

Make letting go and forgiving an ongoing practice. To help with this, remember the following points:

- Controlling the breath controls the mind and emotions—and vice versa.
- Forgive as soon as you realize you have been injured. Don't ignore the fact that you are hurt, but don't get mired in the pain.
- Forgive when you are disappointed or when you feel insulted. Remember how small these things are in the grand scheme of things—mistakes are everywhere.
- Letting go ensures that small irritations do not transform into deeper resentments.
- Forgive when others are uncaring and thoughtless.
- Forgive when you have been injured. Remember, you don't have to relate to the injurer to allow it to happen again—just don't make holding onto the past a detriment to yourself.
- Forgive as often and as quickly as possible.
- Forgive. Forgive it all and move on.

READ THIS WHEN YOU FORGET

- Remember that forgiving is not condoning, trusting, or forgetting.
- Remind yourself that forgiveness is for your own sake—not for those who offended you.
- Remain aware that forgiveness is your responsibility. No one else can or will do it for you.
- You can forgive without the offender's acknowledgement or apology.
- Conflict is an opportunity for you to learn and grow. Practice self-study *(svadhyaya);* give yourself the opportunity to learn whatever you need to learn to leave the past behind.
- Remember the story of Cinderella. Everyone has his or her own perception of how things are. These are neither right nor wrong. They are just different.
- Everyone has positive, wise behavior as well as moments of poor or bad behavior. We tend to judge ourselves by our wise moments and others by their bad moments.
- Remember, we are all human beings, and human beings make mistakes.
- Expectations are hard on relationships. There is no sure way to enforce the empty rules that are a part of the expectation.
- Remember: when reality is better than your expectations, you feel good—and vice versa.

- Accept what is! Reality may not feel good, but it is the only starting place for learning to live a full, free life.
- Expressing anger can relieve some of your pain initially, but negative emotions can be hard on relationships.
- Get objective feedback when you can. Remain open to using that information for your own growth and development.
- Forgiveness is a decision that requires commitment, and this decision must be followed by moment-to-moment choices about how you want to think and feel.
- Remember to forgive yourself.
- Look for the positive in each situation. There is a silver lining. See the benefits inherent in every event.
- Remember the value of focus and detachment. Focus allows you to keep making positive choices. Detachment lets you drop your expectations and live with what is happening.
- Forgiveness comes from working on understanding the situation and your feelings, seeing what you learn, knowing your objectives, committing yourself to happiness, assuming responsibility for your part in a conflict, giving up your own rules and expectations, changing your perspectives, always choosing the positive, and fully committing to the present moment.

READING AND RESOURCES

Forgiveness

Enright, Robert D., Ph.D. *Forgiveness Is a Choice.* Washington, D.C.: American Psychological Association, 2001.

Luskin, Fred, Ph.D. *Forgive for Good: A Proven Prescription for Health and Happiness.* San Francisco: HarperCollins, 2002.

Simon, Sidney B., Ph.D., and Suzanne Simon. *Forgiveness: How to Make Peace with Your Past and Get on with Your Life.* New York: Warner Books, c.1991.

Visualizations

Light Transitions Relaxation/Visualization Tapes. Available online at www.internationalyogastudies.com or call (707) 745-5224.

Shealy, Norman C., M.D., Ph.D. *90 Days to Self-Health.* New York: Dial Press, 1977.

Western Psychology

Gergen, Kenneth J., Ph.D. *An Invitation to Social Construction.* Thousand Oaks, Calif.: SAGE Publications, 1999.

Jampolsky, Gerald, M.D., and Diane Cirincione. *Change Your Mind, Change Your Life: Concepts in Attitudinal Healing.* New York: Bantam, 1993.

Satir, Virginia, M.A., and Michele Baldwin, Ph.D. *Satir Step by Step: A Guide to Creating Change in Families.* Palo Alto, Calif.: Science and Behavior Books, c.1984.

Yoga Philosophy and Psychology

Rama, Swami. *The Art of Joyful Living.* Honesdale, Pa.: Himalayan Institute Press, 2003.

Satchidananda, Sri Swami, translator. *The Yoga Sutras of Patanjali.* Yogaville, Va.: Integral Yoga Publications, 1990.

Tigunait, Pandit Rajmani, Ph.D. *Seven Systems of Indian Philosophy.* Honesdale, Pa.: Himalayan Institute Press, 1983.

Breath Sounds and Relaxation Tapes

Light Transitions Breath Sounds CDs. Available online at www.internatural.com or call (800) 824-6396.

Light Transitions Breath Sounds Tapes. Available online at www.internationalyogastudies.com or call (707) 745-5224.

ABOUT THE AUTHOR

SANDRA SUMMERFIELD KOZAK, M.S., is an internationally celebrated teacher and teacher-trainer who has studied and taught psychology, philosophy, and yoga practice for more than thirty years. She has developed presented accredited university yoga curriculums, nationally televised programs, internationally recognized teacher-training programs, and a variety of seminars and workshops. She teaches monthly workshops throughout America and is regularly invited to teach in Scotland, England, and continental Europe. She received her master's degree from the University of Nevada in health ecology with a minor in psychology. The author of numerous articles, she is the co-author of *Yoga for Your Type: An Ayurvedic Approach to Your Asana Practice* with David Frawley. She lives near San Francisco where she sails, writes, and sees students in private practice.

Kozak is the founder and director of International Yoga

Studies, an internationally affirmed yoga teacher certification program, and the president of Light Transitions, which produces the popular *Breath Sounds* breathing and relaxation tapes. She is an advisory board member of both the Yoga Research Center and *Yoga International* magazine, for which she has been a columnist. She has also served as vice president for both Unity in Yoga and the World Yoga Union.

THE HIMALAYAN INSTITUTE

The main building of the Institute headquarters near Honesdale, Pennsylvania.

FOUNDED IN 1971 BY SWAMI RAMA, the Himalayan Institute has been dedicated to helping people grow physically, mentally, and spiritually by combining the best knowledge of both the East and the West.

Our international headquarters is located on a beautiful 400-acre campus in the rolling hills of the Pocono Mountains of northeastern Pennsylvania. The atmosphere here is one to foster growth, increased inner awareness, and calm. Our grounds provide a wonderfully peaceful and healthy setting for our seminars and extended programs. Students from all over the world join us here to attend programs in such diverse areas as hatha yoga, meditation, stress reduction, ayurveda, nutrition, Eastern philosophy, psychology, and other subjects. Whether the programs are for weekend meditation retreats, week-long seminars on spirituality, months-long residential programs, or holistic health services, the attempt here is to provide an environment of gentle inner progress. We invite you to join with us in the ongoing process of personal growth and development.

The Institute is a nonprofit organization. Your membership in the Institute helps to support its programs. Please call or write for information on becoming a member.

PROGRAMS AND SERVICES INCLUDE:
- Weekend or extended seminars and workshops
- Meditation retreats and advanced meditation instruction
- Hatha yoga teachers' training
- Residential programs for self-development
- Holistic health services and pancha karma at the Institute's Center for Health and Healing
- Spiritual excursions
- Varcho Veda® herbal products
- Himalayan Institute Press
- *Yoga International* magazine
- Sanskrit correspondence course

A Quarterly Guide to Programs and Other Offerings is free within the United States. To request a copy, or for further information, call 800-822-4547 or 570-253-5551; write to the Himalayan Institute, 952 Bethany Turnpike, Honesdale, PA 18431, USA; or visit our Web site at www.HimalayanInstitute.org.

THE HIMALAYAN INSTITUTE PRESS has long been regarded as "The Resource for Holistic Living." We publish dozens of titles, as well as audio- and video-tapes that offer practical methods for living harmoniously and achieving inner balance. Our approach addresses the whole person—body, mind, and spirit—integrating the latest scientific knowledge with ancient healing and self-development techniques.

As such, we offer a wide array of titles on physical and psychological health and well-being, spiritual growth through meditation and other yogic practices, as well as translations of yogic scriptures.

Our yoga accessories include the Japa Kit for meditation practice and the Neti Pot™, the ideal tool for sinus and allergy sufferers. Our Varcho Veda® line of quality herbal extracts is now available to enhance balanced health and well-being.

Subscriptions are available to a bimonthly magazine, *Yoga International,* which offers thought-provoking articles on all aspects of meditation and yoga, including yoga's sister science, ayurveda.

To receive a free catalog, call 800-822-4547 or

570-253-5551; email hibooks@HimalayanInstitute.org; fax 570-647-1552; write to the Himalayan Institute Press, 630 Main St., Suite 350, Honesdale, PA 18431-1843, USA; or visit our Web site at www.HimalayanInstitute.org.